Mastering JavaScript Object-Oriented Programming

Unleash the true power of JavaScript by mastering Object-Oriented programming principles and patterns

Andrea Chiarelli

BIRMINGHAM - MUMBAI

Mastering JavaScript Object-Oriented Programming

First published: June 2016

Production reference: 1220616

Published by Packt Publishing Ltd.
Livery Place
35 Livery Street
Birmingham
B3 2PB, UK.

ISBN 978-1-78588-910-3

www.packtpub.com

Credits

Author

Andrea Chiarelli

Reviewer

Lyubomyr Rudko

Commissioning Editor

Wilson D'souza

Acquisition Editor

Larissa Pinto

Content Development Editor

Shali Deeraj

Technical Editors

Gebin George

Copy Editor

Charlotte Carneiro

Project Coordinator

Sanchita Mandal

Proofreader

Safis Editing

Indexer

Monica Ajmera Mehta

Production Coordinator

Nilesh Mohite

About the Author

Andrea Chiarelli has over 20 years of experience as software engineer and technical writer. Throughout his career, he has used various technologies for the projects he was involved in, ranging from C# to JavaScript, ASP.NET to AngularJS, and REST to PhoneGap/Cordova.

He has contributed to many online and offline magazines, such as *Computer Programming* and *ASP Today* and has coauthored a few books published by Wrox Press.

Currently, he is a senior software engineer at the Italian office of Apparound Inc., a mobile software company founded in the heart of Silicon Valley, and he is a regular contributor to *HTML.it*, an Italian online magazine focused on web technologies. You can contact him at `https://www.linkedin.com/in/andreachiarelli`

I wish to thank my family for their support, patience and love.

About the Reviewer

Lyubomyr Rudko is Senior Software Engineer, and has been developing large web application with JavaScript for the last 6 years. He has great experience in AngularJS, BackboneJS, React.js and Sencha ExtJS. Lyubomyr is a big fan of JavaScript language and truly enjoys sharing his skills and experience with others. Currently, he is working as a Team Technical Lead for Lohika (`http://www.lohika.com/elite-teams/`). You can contact him at `https://ua.linkedin.com/in/lyubomyrrudko`.

www.PacktPub.com

eBooks, discount offers, and more

Did you know that Packt offers eBook versions of every book published, with PDF and ePub files available? You can upgrade to the eBook version at www.PacktPub.com and as a print book customer, you are entitled to a discount on the eBook copy. Get in touch with us at customercare@packtpub.com for more details.

At www.PacktPub.com, you can also read a collection of free technical articles, sign up for a range of free newsletters and receive exclusive discounts and offers on Packt books and eBooks.

https://www2.packtpub.com/books/subscription/packtlib

Do you need instant solutions to your IT questions? PacktLib is Packt's online digital book library. Here, you can search, access, and read Packt's entire library of books.

Why subscribe?

- Fully searchable across every book published by Packt
- Copy and paste, print, and bookmark content
- On demand and accessible via a web browser

Preface

It is now a fact that JavaScript is the most widely used language in the world. Born as a simple glue between the user and the HTML, it has evolved over the years and has acquired an increasingly important role. Today, its scope is no longer just the Web browser, but it lives also on the server, on the desktop PC, on mobile devices up to embedded devices. JavaScript is no longer a simple language to write some scripts, but a language to create complex applications.

Unfortunately, many believe that JavaScript cannot compete with programming languages such as C ++, Java or C #. Many developers with a traditional OOP background think that JavaScript does not have the characteristics to be considered a true Object-Oriented language. This book aims to disprove this prejudice and to show that JavaScript has the characteristics to be considered a true OOP language, although with its peculiarities that make it unique. Thanks to the latest innovations introduced by the ECMAScript standard, we will see how we can write robust and efficient code with JavaScript and we can apply those typical principles of Object-Oriented Programming to create scalable and maintainable applications.

What this book covers

Chapter 1, *A Refresher of Objects*, recalls some basic concepts about objects management in JavaScript covering literal objects, constructor functions and classes.

Chapter 2, *Diving into OOP Principles*, shows that JavaScript supports all the basic principles that allows us to define it a true OOP language.

Chapter 3, *Working with Encapsulation and Information Hiding*, describes some techniques to protect private members of an object, implementing Encapsulation and Information Hiding principles.

Chapter 4, *Inheriting and Creating Mixins*, covers the inheritance mechanism of JavaScript based on prototypes and the creation of mixins.

Chapter 5, *Defining Contracts with Duck Typing*, focuses on using duck typing instead of relying on type checking and shows some techniques to emulate classical OOP interfaces.

Chapter 6, *Advanced Object Creation*, discusses some different ways to create objects and introduces a few Design Patterns such as the Factory Pattern and the Builder Pattern.

Chapter 7, *Presenting Data to the User*, explores the most common Presentation Patterns such as Model View Controller Pattern and Model View ViewModel Pattern.

Chapter 8, *Data Binding*, explains how to implement Data Binding and describes Patterns such as the Observer Pattern and the Publisher/Subscriber Pattern.

Chapter 9, *Asynchronous Programming and Promises*, discusses the issues with asynchronous programming in JavaScript and shows how to overcome them with Promises and other innovative techniques.

Chapter 10, *Organizing Code*, analyzes the various approaches to organize JavaScript code in modules: from the classical IIFE to the latest ECMAScript 6 modules.

Chapter 11, *SOLID Principles*, explores how to apply the five SOLID Design Principles in order to create scalable and maintainable applications.

Chapter 12, *Modern Application Architectures*, describes the most common architectures for JavaScript applications and introduces the Facade and Mediator Patterns.

What you need for this book

Most of the code provided in this book is not bound to a specific JavaScript runtime environment, so it could run in any JavaScript environment. However some examples are specific for the Web browser environment, so the console of Web Inspector such as Chrome Developer tools or Firebug is needed.

Who this book is for

This book is intended for developers with some knowledge and experience in JavaScript that want to deepen the OOP approach.

Conventions

In this book, you will find a number of text styles that distinguish between different kinds of information. Here are some examples of these styles and an explanation of their meaning.

Code words in text, database table names, folder names, filenames, file extensions, pathnames, dummy URLs, user input, and Twitter handles are shown as follows: "Mount the downloaded `WebStorm-10*.dmg` disk image file as another disk in your system."

A block of code is set as follows:

```
var person = {};
person.name = "John";
person.surname = "Smith";
person.address = {
            street: "123 Duncannon Street",
            city: "London",
            country: "United Kingdom"
        };
```

 Warnings or important notes appear in a box like this.

 Tips and tricks appear like this.

For this book we have outlined the shortcuts for the Mac OX platform if you are using the Windows version you can find the relevant shortcuts on the WebStorm help page `https://www.jetbrains.com/webstorm/help/keyboard-shortcuts-by-category.html`.

Reader feedback

Feedback from our readers is always welcome. Let us know what you think about this book-what you liked or disliked. Reader feedback is important for us as it helps us develop titles that you will really get the most out of. To send us general feedback, simply e-mail `feedback@packtpub.com`, and mention the book's title in the subject of your message. If there is a topic that you have expertise in and you are interested in either writing or contributing to a book, see our author guide at `www.packtpub.com/authors`.

Customer support

Now that you are the proud owner of a Packt book, we have a number of things to help you to get the most from your purchase.

Downloading the example code

You can download the example code files for this book from your account at `http://www.packtpub.com`. If you purchased this book elsewhere, you can visit `http://www.packtpub.com/support` and register to have the files e-mailed directly to you.

You can download the code files by following these steps:

1. Log in or register to our website using your e-mail address and password.
2. Hover the mouse pointer on the **SUPPORT** tab at the top.
3. Click on **Code Downloads & Errata**.
4. Enter the name of the book in the **Search** box.
5. Select the book for which you're looking to download the code files.
6. Choose from the drop-down menu where you purchased this book from.
7. Click on **Code Download**.

Once the file is downloaded, please make sure that you unzip or extract the folder using the latest version of:

- WinRAR / 7-Zip for Windows
- Zipeg / iZip / UnRarX for Mac
- 7-Zip / PeaZip for Linux

The code bundle for the book is also hosted on GitHub at `https://github.com/PacktPublishing/Mastering-JavaScript-Object-Oriented-Programming`. We also have other code bundles from our rich catalog of books and videos available at `https://github.com/PacktPublishing/`. Check them out!

Errata

Although we have taken every care to ensure the accuracy of our content, mistakes do happen. If you find a mistake in one of our books-maybe a mistake in the text or the code-we would be grateful if you could report this to us. By doing so, you can save other readers from frustration and help us improve subsequent versions of this book. If you find any errata, please report them by visiting `http://www.packtpub.com/submit-errata`, selecting your book, clicking on the **Errata Submission Form** link, and entering the details of your errata. Once your errata are verified, your submission will be accepted and the errata will be uploaded to our website or added to any list of existing errata under the Errata section of that title.

To view the previously submitted errata, go to `https://www.packtpub.com/books/content/support` and enter the name of the book in the search field. The required information will appear under the **Errata** section.

Piracy

Piracy of copyrighted material on the Internet is an ongoing problem across all media. At Packt, we take the protection of our copyright and licenses very seriously. If you come across any illegal copies of our works in any form on the Internet, please provide us with the location address or website name immediately so that we can pursue a remedy.

Please contact us at `copyright@packtpub.com` with a link to the suspected pirated material.

We appreciate your help in protecting our authors and our ability to bring you valuable content.

Questions

If you have a problem with any aspect of this book, you can contact us at `questions@packtpub.com`, and we will do our best to address the problem.

Table of Contents

1
A Refresher of Objects

Any JavaScript programmer knows that almost everything in this scripting language is an object—from arrays to functions, from regular expressions to dates. We can say that what is not a primitive data type is an object. But, even the primitive data types such as numbers or strings have object wrappers, that is, they are accessible via objects. So, we can argue that objects are vital in JavaScript, and we need to learn the use of objects as best as we can in order to create better applications. One way, for example, to better use objects is applying the **Object-Oriented Programming** (**OOP**) paradigm.

However, before diving into principles and pattern of this programming approach, let's start this first chapter with a quick recap about objects fundamentals. In particular, the chapter will discuss:

- How to create and manage literal objects
- How to define object constructors
- What a prototype is and how to use it
- The new ECMAScript 2015 class construct and its relation to objects, constructors, and prototypes

Object literals

An object is a container of values combined to form a single data structure that has a particular identity. Normally, in fact, an object is used to represent a specific entity such as a person, an order, an invoice, a reservation, and so on, through an aggregation of data and functionalities.

The data is called **properties** and are represented by pairs of names and values. The functionalities are usually called **methods** and are represented by functions, even if they are nothing more than the same pairs of names and values as for properties, where values happen to be functions.

The simplest way to create an object in JavaScript is the literal representation, as shown in the following example:

```
var emptyObject = {};
var person = {"name": "John", "surname": "Smith"};
```

Through the literal notation, we represent an object by enclosing its properties and methods in braces. In the first statement, we created an empty object, an object without properties nor methods; all in all, not very useful but important to understand that an object is basically a list of pairs of values and, as with every list, it can be empty.

In the second declaration, in order to define the object person, we listed two pairs of strings separated by commas. Each pair consists of two strings separated by a colon. The first string is the name of the property while the second one represents its value.

Properties

To assign a name to the properties of an object, we don't have the same restrictions as for the JavaScript variable names. We can use any string, even if there is some constraint when accessing properties with particular names, as we are going to see.

The double or single quotes around the property name are generally optional, but they are required when the name does not follow the rules for variable names. So, we could write our definition of person as follows:

```
var person = {name: "John", surname: "Smith"};
```

But if we want a definition like the following, we are forced to use double or single quotes:

```
var person = {"first-name": "John", "second-name": "Smith"};
```

We can assign any value to an object property and any JavaScript expression, including another object. So, we can create nested objects as shown here:

```
var person = {name: "John",
              surname: "Smith",
              address: {
                street: "13 Duncannon Street",
                city: "London",
```

```
                    country: "United Kingdom"
            }};
```

As we can see, an object with its specific properties is assigned to the `address` property.

To access the values stored in an object property, we have two approaches. The first approach is the so-called **dot-notation,** by which we indicate an object and the property we're interested in, separated by a point:

```
var name = person.name;
```

This is usually the most used approach because it is more compact and quite familiar to developers who have worked with other programming languages.

Using the second approach, we specify the properties of an object by indicating its name as a string in square brackets:

```
var name = person["name"];
```

This approach is mandatory when the property name does not follow the rules for JavaScript's variable names. For example, we cannot use the **dot-notation** to access a property named `first-name`.

If we try to access a non-existing property of an object, an error is not generated but returns the undefined value. In the following example, therefore, the `age` variable will get the *undefined* value:

```
var age = person.age;
```

If we try to assign a value to a not yet defined property, we actually create this property initializing it with the assigned value:

```
person.age = 28;
```

This example shows us the dynamic nature of JavaScript objects. The object's structure is very flexible and can be changed dynamically during the execution of a script. This feature gives us an alternative way for the creation of an object based on a kind of incremental definition. In practice, instead of completely defining a literal representation of our object, we can start from a basic representation and gradually enrich it with the properties we want. Following this approach, we can define our object person as follows:

```
var person = {};
person.name = "John";
person.surname = "Smith";
person.address = {
                street: "123 Duncannon Street",
```

```
                    city: "London",
                    country: "United Kingdom"
                };
    person.age = 28;
```

Besides being able to dynamically create the properties of an object, we can also destroy them at runtime using the `delete` statement. The following example shows how to remove the `address` property from our person object:

```
    delete person.address;
```

After the removal of the `address` property, any attempt to access it will return the value *undefined*.

Methods

While object properties represent data, methods represent actions that an object can perform. From a syntactical point of view, the definition of an object's method is quite similar to the definition of a property. Here's an example:

```
    function showFullName() {
      return "John Smith";
    }

    person.fullName = showFullName;
```

We can also assign a method to an object inside its literal representation as shown here:

```
    var person = {name: "John",
            surname: "Smith",
            showFullName: function() {
              return "John Smith";
            }
    };
```

ECMAScript 2015 allows us to define methods in literal notation in a more direct form, as in the following example:

```
    var person = {name: "John",
            surname: "Smith",
            showFullName() {
              return "John Smith";
            }
    };
```

Actually, the distinction between properties and methods is somewhat artificial in JavaScript. In fact, since the functions are also objects, a method is nothing more than a property that has been assigned a function.

Incidentally, since the value assigned to a property can change at runtime, it is possible that a property, which was initially assigned a function, can then be assigned a different value, such as a string or a number. Unlike other programming languages, a method is not a stable condition for a member of an object, it is not a characteristic of a specific property. We can simply affirm that a property is a method when it has a function assigned, but it is a dynamic condition.

In the previous example, we defined a function that simply returns a string and we assigned that function name to a new property of the person object. Note that we are not assigning the result of the function call to the property, but the function itself by means of its name.

The `fullName` property, since it has been assigned a function, is actually a method. To run it, we must refer to it by specifying parentheses as in a usual function call:

```
var nameAndSurname = person.fullName();
```

Of course, we can assign an anonymous function to a property directly as in the following example:

```
person.fullname = function () {
  return "John Smith";
}
```

The method that we just defined in the example is not so useful. It always displays the same string even if we assign a different value to name and surname of the person object. It would be useful to have a way to display the current value of the corresponding properties.

JavaScript allows us to reach this goal through the *this* keyword. The keyword represents the object when the method is invoked. So, we can rewrite our method in the following way:

```
person.fullName = function () {
  return this.name + " " + this.surname;
};
```

This guarantees the correct display of the current data at the time of the call.

Object constructors

The creation of an object, as we have seen in the examples, is quite straightforward using the literal notation. We do not have to define a class, but we directly create the object just when we need it, and hopefully we can change its structure during the execution of our script.

Suppose, we need multiple objects of the same type, for example more person objects, which share the same structure.

Using the literal notation, we will have to repeat the definition for each object that we want to create, which is essential to identify the single person but unnecessarily repetitive for constant members such as the methods. In other words, using the literal notation in the definition of the objects, we get a non reusable result. For example, if we want to create two person objects, we need to write the following code:

```
var johnSmith = {name: "John",
                 surname: "Smith",
                 address: {
                    street: "13 Duncannon Street",
                    city: "London",
                    country: "United Kingdom"
                 },
                 displayFullName = function() {
                    return this.name + " " + this.surname;
                 }
              };
var marioRossi = {name: "Mario",
                  surname: "Rossi",
                  address: {
                     street: "Piazza Colonna 370",
                     city: "Roma",
                     country: "Italy"
                  },
                  displayFullName = function() {
                     return this.name + " " + this.surname;
                  }
               };
```

Therefore, in order to avoid defining from scratch objects that have the same structure, we can use a **constructor**—a JavaScript function invoked using the new operator. Let's see how to create a constructor for the person object with an example:

```
function Person() {
   this.name = "";
   this.surname = "";
```

```
    this.address = "";
    this.email = "";

    this.displayFullName = function() {...};

}
```

This function defines the properties of our object by assigning them to the `this` keyword and setting default values. Even if this constructor may seem useless since it assigns just empty strings to the properties, it defines a common structure to any object created by it. So, in order to create an object of type `person`, we will have to call the function by prefixing the `new` operator:

```
var johnSmith = new Person();
johnSmith.name = "John";
johnSmith.surname = "Smith";

var marioRossi = new Person();
marioRossi.name = "Mario";
marioRossi.surname = "Rossi";
```

In this way, when we want to create multiple objects with the same structure, we will limit ourselves to just set the specific values that distinguish one object from another.

As you can see, the name given to the constructor is capitalized. This is not a requirement for JavaScript, but a common convention that helps to distinguish regular functions from constructors.

In the definition of a constructor, we can expect the presence of parameters that can be used in the initialization of our object. For example, consider the following definition of the constructor of the person object:

```
function Person(name, surname) {
  this.name = name;
  this.surname = surname;
  this.address = "";
  this.email = "";
  this.displayFullName = function() {...};
}
```

It allows us to create and initialize an object by specifying values directly in the constructor call, as in the following example:

```
var johnSmith = new Persona("John", "Smith");
var marioRossi = new Persona("Mario", "Rossi");
```

It is very important to use the new operator while creating an object through a constructor. In fact, if we forget it, what we get is not the creation of an object, but the execution of the function, with unpredictable results. For example, suppose that we try to create a person object omitting the new operator:

```
var johnSmith = Person();
```

The value of the variable johnSmith will be *undefined*, since the function Person() returns no value. In addition, all the properties and methods defined within the body of the function will be assigned to the object represented by this keyword in the execution context of the function, as can be for example the global object window in a browser. This assignment could redefine the value of variables with the same name causing side effects that are difficult to predict and to debug.

We can reduce the risk of such oversights by resorting to the use of **strict mode**:

```
function Person() {
  "use strict";
  ...
}
```

In *strict mode*, the value of the object represented by the this keyword is *undefined* during the execution of the function. This generates a runtime error while trying to access the property of an object that does not exist, thus avoiding unwanted invocations of the constructor.

Unfortunately, this approach is not sufficient when the constructor is defined inside a namespace:

```
var mankind = {
  ...
  Person: function(name, surname) {
    'use strict';
    this.name = name;
    this.surname = surname;
    ...
  }
};

var johnSmith = mankind.Person("John", "Smith");
```

In this case, the this keyword represents the mankind object, so we will not have a runtime error that warns us of the incorrect use of the constructor, but the properties name and surname will be attached to the mankind object.

The Object() constructor

We have seen how the use of a constructor offers us a higher level of abstraction in the creation of objects. In this section, we explore a particular constructor provided to us by JavaScript—the `Object()` constructor.

This constructor allows us to create a generic object, as shown in the following example:

```
var person = new Object();
person.name = "John";
person.surname = "Smith";
```

Here, we use the `new` operator to create a new instance of an empty object and then we create properties by assigning values, as in the literal approach.

Actually, creating an object using the literal notation or creating it by means of the `Object()` constructor is the same thing. Every object created using the literal notation has `Object()` as its implicit constructor. We can realize it by accessing the `constructor` property that every object has the following:

```
var person = {};
console.log(person.constructor == Object);   //result: true
```

The `Object()` constructor is also able to generate object instances from any JavaScript expression, as shown by the following code:

```
var number = new Object(12);
var anotherNumber = new Object(3*2);
var string = new Object("test");
var person = new Object({name: "John", surname: "Smith"});
```

Apart from the last statement, which is equivalent to the creation of an object via its literal representation, the first three statements create an object from a primitive data type, such as a number or string. The result is not just a numerical value or a string value, but built-in objects specialized in handling numeric values and strings.

We will return later in the book on the `Object()` constructor for use in advanced mode.

Object prototypes

The flexibility of JavaScript objects is expressed primarily through the possibility of changing their structure even after their creation. Even while using a constructor to create an object, we continue to have this possibility. For example, you can write the following code:

```
var johnSmith = new Person("John", "Smith");
var marioRossi = new Person("Mario", "Rossi");

johnSmith.greets = function() {
  console.log("Hello " + this.name + " " + this.surname + "!");
};
```

This code will create a new method `greets()` for the `johnSmith` object without affecting the structure of `marioRossi`.

Basically, while creating objects, we can start from a common structure defined by a constructor and then customize it to our needs.

But how do we change the structure of all objects created using a constructor? For example, suppose that after creating several object using the `Person()` constructor, we want all the `Person` instances to have the `greets()` method. We can do it by exploiting one of the most interesting features of Object-Oriented Programming in JavaScript—the **prototype**.

In our case, we will proceed in the following way:

```
Person.prototype.greets = function() {
  console.log("Hello " + this.name + " " + this.surname + "!");
};
```

This assignment means that all objects created using the `Person()` constructor will instantly have available also the `greets()` method.

To be precise, the new method is not directly attached to each object, but it is accessible as if it were its method. This is possible, thanks to the prototyping mechanism that represents the basis of inheritance in Object-Oriented Programming in JavaScript, as we will discuss later in the book.

In JavaScript, the *prototype* of an object is a kind of reference to another object. The objects we create through the literal notation implicitly refer to *Object* as their prototype.

When we create an object using a constructor, its prototype object is the prototype of the constructor.

If we try to access a property or method of an object that the object itself has not, JavaScript looks for it among the properties and methods of its prototype. So, in our previous example, if we try to access the `greets()` method of the `marioRossi` object, JavaScript does not find it among its methods, but it will find it among the methods of its prototype.

The prototype of an object can in turn have another prototype. In this case, the search for a property or method goes up the prototype chain until you get *object*-the basic prototype of all objects.

JavaScript built-in objects have a prototype reference too. In most cases, their management is quite similar to the prototypes management of objects created through our constructors. This allows us to extend functionality not provided by the built-in objects in a rather simple and elegant way.

For example, if we want to make a padding method available to all strings, we can work on the prototype of the `String()` constructor, as shown here:

```
String.prototype.padLeft = function(width, char) {
  var result = this;
  char = char || " ";

  if (this.length < width)  {
    result = new Array(width - this.length + 1).join(char) + this;
  }
  return result;
};
```

With this definition we can use `padLeft()` as if it were a built-in method of all strings, as shown in the following example:

```
console.log("abc".padLeft(10, "x"));      //"xxxxxxxabc"
```

Using classes

So far, we created objects using two mechanisms: the literal notation and the constructor. These mechanisms let us create objects with a simple approach, without too many formalities.

However, most developers are used to creating objects from the class construct. In fact, many Object-Oriented languages let the developer define classes and create objects as an instance of those classes.

The **ECMAScript 2015** (also known as **ECMAScript 6** or **ES6**) specifications introduce the **class** construct in JavaScript too. However, this construct has nothing to do with the classes of the traditional Object-Oriented Programming paradigm.

While in other languages, such as Java or C#, a class is an abstract description of the structure of an object, in JavaScript the class construct is just a syntactic simplification of the approaches to create objects we have already seen. The JavaScript class construct provides a much simpler and clearer syntax for managing constructors, prototypes, and inheritance.

The new class construct creates order among the different ways of object creation and aims to apply the best practice in prototype management.

Let's take a look at what a class looks like:

```
class Person {
  constructor(name, surname) {
    this.name = name;
    this.surname = surname;
  }
}
```

This class defines a constructor for objects of type `Person`. It is fully equivalent to the following old-style JavaScript code:

```
function Person(name, surname) {
  "use strict";
  this.name = name;
  this.surname = surname;
}
```

We can realize that classes are just syntactic sugar for the constructor's definition, simply getting the type of a class by means of the `typeof` statement:

```
console.log(typeof Person);    //function
```

We can create an object using a class just as we do with constructors, as shown by the following example:

```
var person = new Person("John", "Smith");
```

However, unlike a constructor, we cannot invoke a class like a function, since the following code will raise an exception:

```
var person = Person("John", "Smith");
```

This ensures that we do not run the risk of the side effects that affect traditional constructors.

We can assign a class definition to a variable and then use the variable as an object constructor, as in the following example:

```
var Person = class {
  constructor(name, surname) {
    this.name = name;
    this.surname = surname;
  }
};

var person = new Person("John", "Smith");
```

From a syntactic point of view, a class is a collection of methods included in braces and identified by a name.

One of these methods is the constructor() method, whose task is to define and initialize the properties:

```
class myClass {
  constructor(value1, value2) {
    this.property1 = value1;
    this.property2 = value2;
    this.property3 = "";
  }

  method1() {
    ...
  }

  method2() {
    ...
  }
}
```

The constructor of a class is a method with the reserved name constructor. You cannot have more than one constructor() method in a class.

The constructor method returns, by default, the new instance if it has no return statement, as a common JavaScript constructor. However, it is possible to override the default behavior by inserting a return statement in the constructor body. For example, the following code defines a constructor that returns a literal instance:

```
class myClass {
  constructor(value) {
```

```
        return { property1: value, property2: "" };
    }
}

var x = new myClass("foo");
```

All the methods defined in a class are attached to the prototype property of the class. The prototype property of a class is the prototype that the objects created using this class will have.

The choice to attach methods to the prototype of the class is the result of the application of a common best practice. Since usually methods are not dynamically changed, by attaching them to the prototype, this helps us to optimize memory management. In fact, if methods are not attached to the prototype, then they should be replicated on each newly created object with a proportional need of memory. Attaching methods to the prototype ensures that we have just one copy of them for all objects created from that class.

Unlike functions, classes are not *hoisted*. This means that while a function can be used before its declaration, a class cannot.

So, the following code will raise an exception:

```
var person = new Person();

class Person {...}
```

The features of classes described so far are the basic ones. We will come back to explore other features of new class construct later in the book.

Summary

In this introductory chapter, we recalled some concepts related to object management in JavaScript.

We explored two approaches in creating objects: the literal-based approach and the constructor-based one. The first one is very simple but not practical when we need more generalization, while the second approach is a bit more complex but effective.

We also introduced the new class construct and analyzed how it simplifies the definition of object constructors and the use of prototypes.

In the next chapter, we will analyze how JavaScript applies the Object-Oriented Programming principles.

2
Diving into OOP Principles

In the previous chapter, we introduced objects and their basic use in JavaScript. We have seen that objects have a key role in the language, but many developers consider JavaScript's approach to object management simple compared with the object management of Java, C#, and other OOP languages.

In fact, a common misunderstanding concerns the Object-Oriented nature of JavaScript. Many developers do not consider JavaScript as a true Object-Oriented language, but just a language with an outlandish use of objects.

In this chapter, we will discuss the OOP nature of JavaScript by showing that it complies with the OOP principles. It also will explain the main differences with classical OOP. The following topics will be addressed in the chapter:

- What are the principles of the OOP paradigm?
- Support of abstraction and modeling
- How JavaScript implements Aggregation, Association, and Composition
- The Encapsulation principle in JavaScript
- How JavaScript supports the inheritance principle
- Support of the polymorphism principle
- What the differences are between classical OOP and JavaScript's OOP

OOP principles

OOP is one of the most popular programming paradigms. Many developers use languages based on this programming model such as C++, Java, C#, Smalltalk, Objective-C, and many other. One of the keys to the success of this programming approach is that it promotes a modular design and code reuseâ©©two important features when developing complex software.

However, the OOP paradigm is not based on a formal standard specification. There is not a technical document that defines what OOP is and what it is not. The OOP definition is mainly based on common sense taken from the papers published by early researchers as Kristen Nygaard, Alan Kays, William Cook, and others.

 An interesting discussion about various attempts to define OOP can be found online at the following URL:
`http://c2.com/cgi/wiki?DefinitionsForOo`

Anyway, a widely accepted definition to classify a programming language such as Object Oriented is based on two requirementsâ©©its capability to model a problem through objects and its support of a few principles that grant modularity and code reuse.

In order to satisfy the first requirement, a language must enable a developer to describe the reality using objects and to define relationships among objects such as the following:

- **Association**: This is the object's capability to refer another independent object
- **Aggregation**: This is the object's capability to embed one or more independent objects
- **Composition**: This is the object's capability to embed one or more dependent objects

Commonly, the second requirement is satisfied if a language supports the following principles:

- **Encapsulation**: This is the capability to concentrate into a single entity data and code that manipulates it, hiding its internal details
- **Inheritance**: This is the mechanism by which an object acquires some or all features from one or more other objects
- **Polymorphism**: This is the capability to process objects differently based on their data type or structure

Meeting these requirements is what usually allows us to classify a language as Object Oriented.

Is JavaScript Object Oriented?

Once we have established the principles commonly accepted for defining a language as Object Oriented, can we affirm that JavaScript is an OOP language? Many developers do not consider JavaScript a true object-oriented language due to its lack of class concept and because it does not enforce compliance with OOP principles.

However, we can see that our informal definition make no explicit reference to classes. Features and principles are required for objects. Classes are not a real requirement, but they are sometimes a convenient way to abstract sets of objects with common properties. So, a language can be Object Oriented if it supports objects even without classes, as in JavaScript.

Moreover, the OOP principles required for a language are intended to be supported. They should not be mandatory in order to do programming in a language. The developer can choose to use constructs that allow him to create Object Oriented code or not. Many criticize JavaScript because developers can write code that breaches the OOP principles. But this is just a choice of the programmer, not a language constraint. It also happens with other programming languages, such as C++.

We can conclude that a lack of abstract classes and leaving the developer free to use, or not features that support OOP principles are not real obstacle to consider JavaScript an OOP language. So, let's analyze in the following sections how JavaScript supports abstraction and OOP principles.

Abstraction and modeling support

The first requirement for us to consider a language as Object Oriented is its support to model a problem through objects. We already know that JavaScript supports objects, but here we should determine whether they are supported in order to be able to model reality.

In fact, in Object-Oriented Programming we try to model real-world entities and processes and represent them in our software. We need a model because it is a simplification of reality, it allows us to reduce the complexity offering a vision from a particular perspective and helps us to reason about a relationship among entities.

This simplification feature is usually known as *abstraction*, and it is sometimes considered one of the principles of OOP. Abstraction is the concept of moving the focus from the details and concrete implementation of things to the features that are relevant for a specific purpose, with a more general and abstract approach. In other words, abstraction is the capability to define which properties and actions of a real-world entity have to be represented by means of objects in a program in order to solve a specific problem.

For example, thanks to abstraction, we can decide that to solve a specific problem we can represent a person just as an object with name, surname, and age, since other information such as address, height, hair color, and so on are not relevant for our purpose.

More than a language feature, it seems a human capability. For this reason, we prefer not to consider it an OOP principle but a (human) capability to support modeling.

Modeling reality not only involves defining objects with relevant features for a specific purpose. It also includes the definition of relationships between objects, such as Association, Aggregation, and Composition.

Association

Association is a relationship between two or more objects where each object is independent of each other. This means that an object can exist without the other and no object owns the other.

Let us clarify with an example. In order to define a parent-child relationship between persons, we can do so as follows:

```
function Person(name, surname) {
this.name = name;
this.surname = surname;
this.parent = null;
}

var johnSmith = new Person("John", "Smith");
var fredSmith = new Person("Fred", "Smith");

fredSmith.parent = johnSmith;
```

The assignment of the object `johnSmith` to the `parent` property of the object `fredSmith` establishes an association between the two objects. Of course, the object `johnSmith` lives independently from the object `fredSmith` and vice versa. Both can be created and deleted independently to each other.

As we can see from the example, JavaScript allows us to define association between objects using a simple object reference through a property.

Aggregation

Aggregation is a special form of association relationship where an object has a major role than the other one. Usually, this major role determines a sort of ownership of an object in relation to the other. The owner object is often called *aggregate* and the owned object is called *component*. However, each object has an independent life.

An example of an aggregation relationship is the one between a company and its employees, as in the following example:

```
var company = {
    name: "ACME Inc.",
    employees: []
};

var johnSmith = new Person("John", "Smith");
var marioRossi = new Person("Mario", "Rossi");

company.employees.push(johnSmith);
company.employees.push(marioRossi);
```

The person objects added to the `employees` collection help define the company object, but they are independent from it. If the company object is deleted, each single person still lives. However, the real meaning of a company is bound to the presence of its employees.

Again, the code show us that the aggregation relationship is supported by JavaScript by means of object reference.

It is important not to confuse the Association with the Aggregation. Even if the support of the two relationships is syntactically identical, that is, the assignment or attachment of an object to a property, from a conceptual point of view they represent different situations.

Aggregation is the mechanism that allows you to create an object consisting of several objects, while the association relates autonomous objects.

In any case, JavaScript makes no control over the way in which we associate or aggregate objects between them. Association and Aggregation raise a constraint more conceptual than technical.

Composition

Composition is a strong type of Aggregation, where each component object has no independent life without its owner, the aggregate. Consider the following example:

```
var person = {name: "John",
              surname: "Smith",
              address: {
                street: "123 Duncannon Street",
                city: "London",
                country: "United Kingdom"
              }};
```

This code defines a person with his address represented as an object. The `address` property is strictly bound to the `person` object. Its life is dependent on the life of the person and it cannot have an independent life without the person. If the `person` object is deleted, also the `address` object is deleted.

In this case, the strict relation between the person and their address is expressed in JavaScript assigning directly the literal representing the address to the `address` property.

OOP principles support

The second requirement that allows us to consider JavaScript as an Object-Oriented language involves the support of at least three principlesâ⊙⊙encapsulation, inheritance, and polymorphism. Let analyze how JavaScript supports each of these principles.

Encapsulation

Objects are central to the Object-Oriented Programming model, and they represent the typical expression of *encapsulation*, that is, the ability to concentrate in one entity both data (properties) and functions (methods), hiding the internal details.

In other words, the encapsulation principle allows an object to expose just what is needed to use it, hiding the complexity of its implementation. This is a very powerful principle, often found in the real world that allows us to use an object without knowing how it internally works. Consider for instance how we drive cars. We need just to know how to speed up, brake, and change direction. We do not need to know how the car works in detail, how its motor burns fuel or transmits movement to the wheels.

To understand the importance of this principle also in software development, consider the following code:

```
var company = {
    name: "ACME Inc.",
    employees: [],
    sortEmployeesByName: function() {...}
};
```

It creates a `company` object with a name, a list of employees and a method to sort the list of employees using their name property. If we need to get a sorted list of employees of the company, we simply need to know that the `sortEmployeesByName()` method accomplishes this task. We do not need to know how this method works, which algorithm it implements. That is an implementation detail that encapsulation hides from us.

Hiding internal details and complexity has two main reasons:

- The first reason is to provide a simplified and understandable way to use an object without the need to understand the complexity inside. In our example, we just need to know that to sort employees, we have to call a specific method.
- The second reason is to simplify change management. Changes to the internal sort algorithm do not affect our way to order employees by name. We always continue to call the same method. Maybe we will get a more efficient execution, but the expected result will not change.

We said that encapsulation hides internal details in order to simplify both the use of an object and the change of its internal implementation. However, when internal implementation depends on publicly accessible properties, we risk to frustrate the effort of hiding internal behavior. For example, what happens if you assign a string to the property `employees` of the object `company`?

```
company.employees = "this is a joke!";

company.sortEmployeesByName();
```

The assignment of a string to a property whose value is an array is perfectly legal in JavaScript, since it is a language with dynamic typing. But most probably, we will get an exception when calling the sort method after this assignment, since the sort algorithm expects an array.

In this case, the encapsulation principle has not been completely implemented. A general approach to prevent direct access to relevant properties is to replace them with methods. For example, we can redefine our company object as in the following:

```
function Company(name) {
    var employees = [];

    this.name = name;

        this.getEmployees = function() {
            return employees;
            };
    this.addEmployee = function(employee) {
            employees.push(employee);
            };
    this.sortEmployeesByName = function() {
            ...
            };
}

var company = new Company("ACME Inc.");
```

With this approach, we cannot access directly the `employees` property, but we need to use the `getEmployees()` method to obtain the list of employees of the company and `addEmployee()` to add an employee to the list. This guarantees that the internal state remains really hidden and consistent. The way we created methods for the `Company()` constructor is not the best one. We will see why and how to use a better approach in `Chapter 3`, *Working with Encapsulation and Information Hiding*.

This is just one possible approach to enforce encapsulation by protecting the internal state of an object. This kind of data protection is usually called *information hiding* and, although often linked to encapsulation, it should be considered as an autonomous principle. Information hiding deals with the accessibility to an object's members, in particular to properties. While encapsulation concerns hiding details, the information hiding principle usually allows different access levels to the members of an object.

We will discuss more in deep encapsulation and information hiding in the next chapter, since different solutions can be applied in JavaScript in order to emulate the common access levels supported by other OOP languages.

Inheritance

OOP, inheritance enables new objects to acquire the properties of existing objects. This relationship between two objects is very common and can be found in many situations in real life. It usually refers to creating a specialized object starting from a more general one.

In OOP, inheritance enables new objects to acquire the properties of existing objects. This relationship between two objects is very common and can be found in many situations in real life. It usually refers to creating a specialized object starting from a more general one. Let's consider, for example, a person: he has some features such as name, surname, height, weight, and so on. This set of features describes a generic entity that represents a person. Using abstraction, we can select the features needed for our purpose and represent a person as an object:

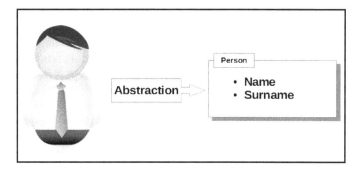

If we need a special person who is able to program computers, that is a programmer, we need to create an object that has all the properties of a generic person plus some new properties that characterize the programmer object. For instance, the new programmer object can have a property describing which programming language they know.

Suppose we choose to create the new programmer object by duplicating the properties of the person object and adding to it the programming language knowledge as follows:

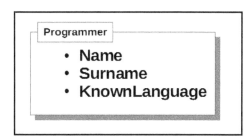

This approach is in contrast with the Object-Oriented Programming goals. In particular, it does not reuse existing code, since we are duplicating the properties of the person object. A more appropriate approach should reuse the code created to define the person object. This is where the inheritance principle can help us. It allows us to share common features between objects, avoiding code duplication:

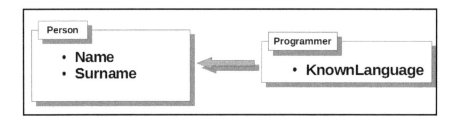

 Inheritance is also called *subclassing* in languages that support classes. A class that inherits from another class is called a *subclass*, while the class from which it is derived is called a *superclass*. Apart from the naming, the inheritance concept is the same, although of course it does not seem suited to JavaScript.

We can implement inheritance in JavaScript in various ways. Consider, for example, the following constructor of person objects:

```
function Person() {
this.name = "";
this.surname = "";
}
```

In order to define a programmer as a person specialized in computer programming, we will add a new property describing its knowledge about a programming language: knownLanguage.

A simple approach to create the programmer object that inherits properties from person is based on prototype. Here is a possible implementation:

```
function Programmer() {
    this.knownLanguage = "";
}

Programmer.prototype = new Person();
```

We will create a programmer with the following code:

```
var programmer = new Programmer();
```

We will obtain an object that has the properties of the person object (`name` and `surname`) and the specific property of the programmer (`knownLanguage`), that is, the programmer object inherits the person properties.

This is a simple example to demonstrate that JavaScript supports the inheritance principle of Object-Oriented Programming at its basic level. Inheritance is a complex concept that has many facets and several variants in programming, many of them dependent on the used language.

In `Chapter 4`, *Inheriting and Creating Mixins*, we will explore more in depth how JavaScript supports inheritance, analyzing different approaches and more advanced topics such as overriding and multiple inheritance.

Polymorphism

In Object-Oriented Programming, polymorphism is understood in different ways, even if the basis is a common notionâ©©the ability to handle multiple data types uniformly.

Support of polymorphism brings benefits in programming that go toward the overall goal of OOP. Mainly, it reduces coupling in our application, and in some cases, allows to create more compact code.

The most common ways to support polymorphism with a programming language include:

- Methods that take parameters with different data types (overloading)
- Management of generic types, not known in advance (parametric polymorphism)
- Expressions whose type can be represented by a class and classes derived from it (*subtype polymorphism* or *inclusion polymorphism*)

In most languages, *overloading* is what happens when you have two methods with the same name but different signatures. At compile time, the compiler works out which method to call based on matching between types of invocation arguments and method's parameters. The following is an example of method overloading in C#:

```
public int CountItems(int x) {
    return x.ToString().Length;
}

public int CountItems(string x) {
    return x.Length;
}
```

The `CountItems()` method has two signaturesâ©©one for integers and one for strings. This allows to count the number of digits in a number or the number of characters in a string in a uniform manner, just calling the same method.

Overloading can also be expressed through methods with different numbers of arguments, as shown in the following C# example:

```
public int Sum(int x, int y) {
    return Sum(x, y, 0);
}

public int Sum(int x, int y, int z) {
    return x+ y + z;
}
```

Here, we have the `Sum()` method that is able to sum two or three integers. The correct method definition will be detected on the basis of the number of arguments passed.

As JavaScript developers, we are able to replicate this behavior in our scripts. For example, the C# `CountItems()` method becomes in JavaScript as follows:

```
function countItems(x) {
return x.toString().length;
}
```

While the `Sum()` example will be as follows:

```
function sum(x, y, z) {
x = x?x:0;
y = y?y:0;
z = z?z:0;
return x + y + z;
}
```

Or, using the more convenient ES6 syntax:

```
function sum(x = 0, y = 0, z = 0) {
return x + y + z;
}
```

These examples demonstrate that JavaScript supports overloading in a more immediate way than strong-typed languages.

In strong-typed languages, overloading is sometimes called *static polymorphism*, since the correct method to invoke is detected statically by the compiler at compile time. This is opposed to *dynamic polymorphism* that concerns method overriding, as we will see in a later chapter.

Parametric polymorphism allows a method to work on parameters of any type. Often it is also called **generics** and many languages support it in built-in methods. For example, in C#, we can define a list of items whose type is not defined in advance using the List<T> generic type. This allows us to create lists of integers, strings, or any other type.

We can also create our generic class as shown by the following C# code:

```
public class Stack<T> {
    private T[] items;
    private int count;
    public void Push(T item) { ... }
    public T Pop() { ... }
}
```

This code defines a typical stack implementation whose item's type is not defined. We will be able to create, for example, a stack of strings with the following code:

```
var stack = new Stack<String>();
```

Due to its dynamic data typing, JavaScript supports parametric polymorphism implicitly. In fact, the type of function's parameters is inherently generic, since its type is set when a value is assigned to it. The following is a possible implementation of a stack constructor in JavaScript:

```
function Stack()
{
 this.stack = [];
 this.pop = function(){
  return this.stack.pop();
 }
 this.push = function(item){
  this.stack.push(item);
 }
}
```

Subtype polymorphism allows the consideration of objects of different types, but with an inheritance relationship, to be handled consistently. This means that wherever I can use an object of a specific type, here I can use an object of a type derived from it.

Let's see a C# example to clarify this concept:

```
public class Person {
 public string Name {get; set;}
 public string SurName {get; set;}
}

public class Programmer:Person {
    public String KnownLanguage {get; set;}
}

public void WriteFullName(Person p) {
 Console.WriteLine(p.Name + " " + p.SurName);
}

var a = new Person();
a.Name = "John";
a.SurName = "Smith";

var b = new Programmer();
b.Name = "Mario";
b.SurName = "Rossi";
b.KnownLanguage = "C#";

WriteFullName(a);    //result: John Smith
WriteFullName(b);    //result: Mario Rossi
```

In this code, we again present the definition of the `Person` class and its derived class `Programmer` and define the method `WriteFullName()` that accepts argument of type `Person`. Thanks to subtype polymorphism, we can pass to `WriteFullName()` also objects of type `Programmer`, since it is derived from `Person`. In fact, from a conceptual point of view a programmer is also a person, so subtype polymorphism fits to a concrete representation of reality.

Of course, the C# example can be easily reproduced in JavaScript since we have no type constraint. Let's see the corresponding code:

```
function Person() {
this.name = "";
this.surname = "";
}

function Programmer() {
    this.knownLanguage = "";
}

Programmer.prototype = new Person();
```

```
function writeFullName(p) {
    console.log(p.name + " " + p.surname);
}

var a = new Person();
a.name = "John";
a.surname = "Smith";

var b = new Programmer();
b.name = "Mario";
b.surname = "Rossi";
b.knownLanguage = "JavaScript";

writeFullName(a);    //result: John Smith
writeFullName(b);    //result: Mario Rossi
```

As we can see, the JavaScript code is quite similar to the C# code and the result is the same.

JavaScript OOP versus classical OOP

The discussion conducted so far shows how JavaScript supports the fundamental OOP principles and can be considered a true OOP language as many others. However, JavaScript differs from most other languages for certain specific features which can create some concern to the developers used to working with programming languages that implement the classical OOP.

The first of these features is the dynamic nature of the language both in data type management and object creation. Since data types are dynamically evaluated, some features of OOP, such as polymorphism, are implicitly supported. Moreover, the ability to change an object structure at runtime breaks the common sense that binds an object to a more abstract entity such as a class.

The lack of the concept of class is another big difference with the classical OOP. Of course, we are talking about the class generalization, nothing to do with the class construct introduced by ES6 that represents just a syntactic convenience for standard JavaScript constructors.

Classes in most Object-Oriented languages represent a *generalization* of objects, that is, an extra level of abstraction upon the objects.

So, classical Object-Oriented programming has two types of abstractions—classes and objects. An object is an abstraction of a real-world entity while a class is an abstraction of an object or another class (in other words, it is a generalization). Objects in classical OOP languages can only be created by instantiating classes.

JavaScript has a different approach to object management. It has just one type of abstraction—the objects. Unlike the classical OOP approach, an object can be created directly as an abstraction of a real-world entity or as an abstraction of another object. In the latter case the abstracted object is called prototype. As opposed to the classical OOP approach, the JavaScript approach is sometimes called *Prototypal Object-Oriented Programming*.

Of course, the lack of a notion of class in JavaScript affects the inheritance mechanism. In fact, while in classical OOP inheritance is an operation allowed on classes, in prototypal OOP inheritance is an operation on objects.

That does not mean that classical OOP is better than prototypal OOP or vice versa. They are simply different approaches. However, we cannot ignore that these differences lead to some impact in the way we manage objects. At least we note that while in classical OOP classes are immutable, that is we cannot add, change, or remove properties or methods at runtime, in prototypal OOP objects and prototypes are extremely flexible. Moreover, classical OOP adds an extra level of abstraction with classes, leading to a more verbose code, while prototypal OOP is more immediate and requires a more compact code.

Summary

In this chapter, we explored the basic principles of the OOP paradigm. We have been focusing on abstraction to define objects, association, aggregation, and composition to define relationships between objects, encapsulation, inheritance, and polymorphism principles to outline the basic principles required by OOP. We have seen how JavaScript supports all features that allow us to define it as a true OOP language and have compared classical OOP with prototypal OOP.

Once we established that JavaScript is a true Object-Oriented language like other languages such as Java, C #, and C ++, we will continue in the coming chapters by exploring how to take advantage of OOP support for our applications. In particular, in the next chapter we will focus on encapsulation and information hiding, analyzing the advanced JavaScript support and the most common patterns.

3
Working with Encapsulation and Information Hiding

In this chapter, we will explore the relationship between encapsulation and information hiding, and we will see the different approaches to implement the visibility and accessibility of members of a JavaScript object. The following topics will be addressed in this chapter:

- Public and private properties
- Scope and closure
- Techniques to protect private members
- Getters, setters, and property descriptors
- Property definition in ES6 classes

Encapsulation and information hiding

Encapsulation is one of the basic principles of the OOP paradigm. It allows us to bundle it into one object both data and functionalities that operate on that data.

Using the methods exposed by the object to manipulate the data, we take advantage of the encapsulation principle ignoring its internal complexity and implementation details. In other words, encapsulation hides the internal details regarding how the object manipulates its data. This feature, called the information hiding principle, is often related to encapsulation, although it is a more general principle. By hiding internal details, we obtain at least two great benefits:

- We provide a simple way to use an object, hiding the internal complexity
- We decouple the internal implementation from the use of the object, simplifying change management

The information hiding principle enforces the design of objects to have at least two parts: a public part and a private one. Only the public part is accessible by clients that want to interoperate with the object.

Many object-oriented languages, such as Java and C#, provide specific keywords such as *public* and *private* (**access modifiers**) to allow developers to easily implement the Information Hiding principle. JavaScript does not include such keywords. All members in an object are public by default. However, some common patterns can be used to obtain different levels of information hiding as happens in most classical OOP languages.

Convention-based approach

JavaScript objects do not care about privacy. All the properties and methods are publicly accessible if no caution is taken. So, if we want to avoid access to some properties or methods concerning internal implementation details, we have to set up a strategy.

A first simple approach consists in adopting convention-based naming for internal members of an object. For example, internal members can have a name starting with a prefix, such as the underscore (_) character. Let's explain with an example:

```
function TheatreSeats() {
  this._seats = [];
}

TheatreSeats.prototype.placePerson = function(person) {
  this._seats.push(person);
};
```

This code defines a constructor for objects that represent seats in a theatre where a person can be placed. The intended use is as follows:

```
var theatreSeats = new TheatreSeats();

theatreSeats.placePerson({name: "John", surname: "Smith"});
```

The _seats property is the actual container and its underscore character prefix indicates that it should be considered an internal property. Of course, it is just a convention—the developer should know that members of an object whose names start with the underscore character are for internal use.

However, there is no technical obstacle to prevent a developer using that member. The internal details are not really hidden and privacy is based on the developer's willingness. Apart from this, the convention—based approach has some other drawbacks. For example, it pollutes the public interface with members that should not be used, breaking the principle that using an object should be simple. Moreover, it can lead to property clashes when using inheritance.

Even if this approach can appear simple, it has been widely used by common JavaScript libraries such as *jQuery* and *Backbone.js*.

Privacy levels using closure

A simple way to fix the inconsistencies of the convention-based approach is not using properties for internal members but declaring variables inside the constructor, as shown in the following example:

```
function TheatreSeats() {
  var seats = [];

  this.placePerson = function(person) {
    seats.push(person);
  };
}
```

Using this approach, we can continue to use the constructor as usual preventing the access to the actual internal container-the `seats` variable. We are exploiting the internal environment of the `TheatreSeats()` function to hide the implementation details and lay the foundations for building the private and public parts of JavaScript objects.

Scope and closure

Before going further, it is useful to make clear some concepts that are used very often in JavaScript programming and on which we will build our approach to implement the information hiding principle. Let's start with the following example:

```
var greeting = "Good morning";

function greets(person) {

  var fullName = person.name + " " + person.surname;

  function displayGreeting() {
    console.log(greeting + " " + fullName);
  }

  displayGreeting();
}

greets({name: "John", surname: "Smith"});
```

We defined the `greets()` function that takes a person object as argument and displays a string resulting from the concatenation of the greeting with the full name of the person. The actual function displaying the greeting is the `displayGreeting()` function defined inside the body of `greets()` function.

We already know that a variable or argument has a visibility scope that is a context inside which it is accessible. Each function creates its own scope, variables, parameters, or functions defined inside the body of a function are not accessible by code outside its body. The code of a function can access variables defined in the function's scope, but it can also access variables defined in the outer scope, that is, the external context that contains the function.

This led us to think of scopes as nested containers where the inner container can access the outer container, but not vice versa. This is usually known as the **scope chain**. The following picture shows how we can graphically represent the scope chain of our example:

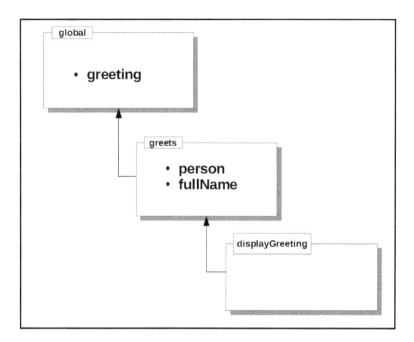

As a general rule, when a statement refers to a variable, it is searched in the current scope, if it is not found, it is searched in the outer scope and so on until it is found or the global scope is reached. So, in our example, the reference to the greeting variable inside the displayGreeting() function is first searched inside the function scope itself. Since it is not defined here, it is searched in the outer scope, that is, the scope of greets() function. Again, since the greeting variable is not defined here, it is searched and found in the outer scope that is the global scope.

The interesting side of this mechanism is that, in JavaScript, it is possible to access the outer scope even when the function that created it has terminated. To better explain, rewrite the previous code as follows:

```
var greeting = "Good morning";
var displayGreeting;

function greets(person) {

  var fullName = person.name + " " + person.surname;


  return function () {
    console.log(greeting + " " + fullName);
  }
```

```
  }

  displayGreeting = greets({name: "John", surname: "Smith"});

  displayGreeting();
```

In this case, the `greets()` function does not shows the greeting string, but it returns a function that is able to show the string. We assigned the result of the `greets()` function to the variable `displayGreeting` and called the function it contains. We will get again the greeting string as before. Even if the execution context of the `greets()` function does not exist anymore, the resulting function can still access its scope, in particular the `fullName` variable.

The basic principle strengthening this mechanism establishes that each variable that was accessible when a function was defined is *enclosed* in the accessible scope of the function. This mechanism is called **closure**.

The closure is a powerful tool and can be creatively used to define patterns of advanced programming, as we will see throughout the book. We will use it in this chapter to implement information hiding. Let's recall the previous example of our constructor definition:

```
  function TheatreSeats() {
    var seats = [];

    this.placePerson = function(person) {
      seats.push(person);
    };
  }
```

When this constructor is invoked to create an object, the constructor's instance and its internal environment are created. The constructor's environment holds the parameters, the local variables, and functions created inside the constructor. These functions will retain a reference to the environment in which they were created so that they will always have access to the environment, even after the constructor execution terminates. This combination of function and environment, that is the closure, represents thus a data storage that is independent of the instance and related to it only because the two are created at the same time.

Privacy levels

Therefore, exploiting the closure of a constructor we can implement the information hiding principle for JavaScript objects. As we can see, however, the new definition of the `TheatreSeats()` constructor is slightly different from the original one. While in the original definition we attached the `placePerson()` method to the prototype of the constructor, now we cannot follow this approach. In fact, the prototype's methods cannot access the constructor's closure, so the following code cannot work:

```
function TheatreSeats() {
  var seats = [];
}

TheatreSeats.prototype.placePerson = function(person) {
  seats.push(person);
};

var theatreSeats = new TheatreSeats();

theatreSeats.placePerson({name: "John", surname: "Smith"});    //exception
```

The last statement in the previous example raises an exception because the `placePerson()` method tries to access a `seats` variable that is not defined in its execution context. So, in order to use the constructor's closure to hide the internal details, we need to implement a method inside the constructor itself.

This led us to apply a sort of classification of an object's members in order to determine how to implement the information hiding principle:

- Members that cannot be publicly accessed (**private members**)
- Members that do not use private members and that can be publicly accessed (**public members**)
- Members that use private members and that can be publicly accessed (**privileged members**)

 The privacy levels terminology has been defined by Douglas Cockford in his article at `http://www.crockford.com/javascript/private.htm` `l`.

This classification defines three **privacy levels**, and it requires us to use different approaches to implement them in a JavaScript object:

- A private member must be implemented as a local variable or function of the constructor
- A public member must be implemented as a member of `this` keyword, if it is a property, or as a member of the constructor's prototype, if it is a method
- A privileged member must be implemented as a member of `this` keyword inside the constructor

The following code shows a version of the `TheatreSeats()` constructor that implements the three privacy levels:

```
function TheatreSeats() {
  var seats = [];

  this.placePerson = function(person) {
    seats.push(person);
  };
  this.countOccupiedSeats = function() {
    return seats.length;
  };

  this.maxSize = 10;
}

TheatreSeats.prototype.isSoldOut = function() {
  return this.countOccupiedSeats () >= this.maxSize;
};

TheatreSeats.prototype.countFreeSeats = function() {
  return this.maxSize - this.countOccupiedSeats();
};
```

As we know, the `seats` variable is a private member, and it is not accessible from outside the constructor's closure. The `placePerson()` and `countOccupiedSeats()` methods are privileged members, since they can access the private variable `seats`. The `maxSize` property and the `isSoldOut()` and `countFreeSeats()` methods are public members since they do not directly access private members. However, they access the `seats` variable indirectly through the privileged methods.

Benefits and drawbacks

Compared to the convention-based approach, the use of closure to define the three levels of privacy is much more effective. It actually grants private data protection and exposes just what the developers needs to access to use the object. However, this solution suffers from some flaws.

The first point is purely formal. Both privileged methods and private functions break the separation of concerns between the constructor and the instance prototype of an object. In fact, the constructor should be responsible for data initialization of an object instance. The prototype should be responsible for general methods definitions and shared functionalities. By defining methods inside the constructor, we are giving it a responsibility for which it has not been designed.

Another drawback regards memory consumption. By attaching a method to the prototype of a constructor, we share the functionality among all instances created by the constructor. The prototype mechanism grants us just one copy of the method definition that exists in the application. Instead, each privileged method definition is replicated for each object instance, unnecessarily increasing memory consumption.

In order to mitigate memory consumption, we can choose to define a minimum set of privileged methods and to delegate to public methods those functionalities resulting from the composition of privileged methods. We used this approach for the `isSoldOut()` and `countFreeSeats()` methods definition. Although this expedient allows us to reduce memory consumption, we will have some loss in performance due to indirect access to the constructor's closure as a counterpart.

A meta-closure approach

The basic idea of the previous approach builds on the nature of closure. The constructor's environment is protected by default and remains accessible from the inside of the constructor itself even after it terminates. However, since the closure is created when the constructor is called, each object instance needs to have both private data and privileged methods defined inside the constructor context. An ideal solution should be one that protects private data letting them be accessible from outside the constructor's closure. This should be a sort of meta-closure that offers an extra level of protection-a closure accessible from outside the object constructor by prototype members still hiding private data of the resulting object. This meta—closure can be built using an **Immediately Invoked Function Expression (IIFE)**.

Immediately invoked function expressions

An IIFE, also called a **self-executing anonymous function**, is a JavaScript expression involving an anonymous function definition immediately executed. The following is a minimal example of such an expression:

```
var value = function() { return 3 + 2; }();
```

We can see that it consists of a standard anonymous function definition followed by the invocation operator (). At first glance, it may seem a weird expression; but if we reason a moment, we find that it is less strange than it seems. In fact, since in JavaScript functions are also object, we can assign them to variables. For example, we can write the following assignment:

```
var aFunction = function() { return 3 + 2; };
```

Then, we can call the function by simply attaching the () operator at the end of the variable:

```
var value = aFunction();
```

The IIFE simply composes these two steps into one assignment.

But, how can an IIFE help us in protecting data privacy allowing privileged methods to be defined outside the constructor? IIFE expressions involve function definitions, and like any function definition, they build closures. If we combine the ability of a JavaScript function to return another function, we create nested closures that bring us closer to our solution.

Creating a meta-closure with an IIFE

Let's rewrite our TheatreSeats() constructor using an IIFE. The following may be an example of such rewriting:

```
var  TheatreSeats = (function() {
  var seats = [];

  function TheatreSeatsConstructor() {
    this.maxSize = 10;
  }

  TheatreSeatsConstructor.prototype.placePerson = function(person)    {
    seats.push(person);
  };

  TheatreSeatsConstructor.prototype.countOccupiedSeats =    function() {
```

```
      return seats.length;
  };

  TheatreSeatsConstructor.prototype.isSoldOut = function() {
    return seats.length >= this.maxSize;
  };

  TheatreSeatsConstructor.prototype.countFreeSeats = function() {
    return this.maxSize - seats.length;
  };

  return  TheatreSeatsConstructor;

}());
```

The code assigns the result of an IIFE to the `TheatreSeats` variable. The anonymous function declares in its local scope the `seats` array and the `TheatreSeatsConstructor()` constructor and attaches all methods to the prototype of the constructor. It then returns the constructor itself. As a result, the `TheatreSeats` variable will contain our final constructor.

With this approach, the methods attached to the constructor's prototype can still access the private array `seats`, since it is part of the closure of the anonymous function. This finally allows us to bring privileged methods definition outside the constructor scope, sharing them among the object instances.

However, this approach still has an annoying problem. Since the `seats` array belongs to the anonymous function's closure, it is shared among all object instances created using the `TheatreSeats()` constructor. We can verify it by executing the following code:

```
var t1 = new TheatreSeats();
var t2 = new TheatreSeats();

t1.placePerson({name: "John", surname: "Smith"});

console.log(t1.countFreeSeats());    //result: 9
console.log(t2.countFreeSeats());    //result: 9
```

We created two instances of `TheatreSeats` objects and placed one person on the first object. By calling the `countFreeSeats()` method of the first instance, we correctly get 9 free seats. However, by calling the same method of the second instance, we get the same result as well, even if we did not place a person on it.

Since the `seat` array is shared among all instances, any change to it is available to other instances. Technically, we created a **static local variable**. In some contexts it could be desirable, but not in this one.

Managing isolated private members

A way to bypass the problem of static private members creation is to identify each object instance and attach to it its private set of data. Consider the following code:

```
var  TheatreSeats = (function() {
  var priv = {};
  var id = 0;

  function TheatreSeatsConstructor() {
    this.id = id++;
    this.maxSize = 10;

    priv[this.id] = {};
    priv[this.id].seats = [];
  }

  TheatreSeatsConstructor.prototype.placePerson = function(person)    {
    priv[this.id].seats.push(person);
  };

  TheatreSeatsConstructor.prototype.countOccupiedSeats =    function() {
    return priv[this.id].seats.length;
  };

  TheatreSeatsConstructor.prototype.isSoldOut = function() {
    return priv[this.id].seats.length >= this.maxSize;
  };

  TheatreSeatsConstructor.prototype.countFreeSeats = function() {
    return this.maxSize - priv[this.id].seats.length;
  };

  return  TheatreSeatsConstructor;

}());
```

We highlighted the main differences with the previous version of the code. In this case, we declared two variables in the scope of the anonymous function: `priv` and `id`. The former is an object that will contain the private members of each object instance, the latter will contain a numeric identifier that will be attached to each object instance. These variables will be available in the closure of the anonymous function so that they will be static variables shared among all object instances.

When the constructor is called, it creates an extra property `id` with the next value of the `id` variable. Then, it uses this `id` property as the key to create and access the private members attached to the `priv` object. This means that wherever we made reference to the `seats` array, we will refer to `priv[this.id].seats`.

This technique resolves the static variable problem, but still has a couple of problems.

The first problem concerns the new `id` property. We need this property in order to identify each object instance and to access its private members. However, since it is a publicly accessible number, it represents a potential risk. If we change its value, even if accidentally, we incur unexpected behavior.

The second problem regards again memory consumption. Since private members exist in the meta-closure, their life will coincide with the closure life. So, if we create an object using our constructor and then destroy the object, its private members will remain alive in the anonymous function's closure, wasting memory. No garbage collector will remove these members since it is not aware that they are not used.

A definitive solution with WeakMaps

Both problems affecting the isolated closure approach can be finally resolved using a new ECMAScript 6 feature—the **WeakMap**. A WeakMap is a collection of key and value pairs where the key must be an object. In the following example, we build a WeakMap with two items:

```
var myMap = new WeakMap();
var johnSmith = {name: "John", surname: "Smith"};
var marioRossi = {name: "Mario", surname: "Rossi"};


myMap.set(johnSmith, "This is John");
myMap.set(marioRossi, "This is Mario");

console.log(myMap.get(marioRossi));
```

We used the `set()` method to define an association between an object and another item (a string in our case). We used the `get()` method to retrieve the item associated with an object. The interesting aspect of the WeakMaps is the fact that it holds a **weak** reference to the key inside the map. A weak reference means that if the object is destroyed, the garbage collector will remove the entire entry from the WeakMap, thus freeing up memory.

Let's use WeakMaps to solve our problems:

```
var  TheatreSeats = (function() {
  var priv = new WeakMap();

  function TheatreSeatsConstructor() {
    var privateMembers = {seats: []};
    priv.set(this, privateMembers);

    this.maxSize = 10;

  }

  TheatreSeatsConstructor.prototype.placePerson = function(person)    {
    priv.get(this).seats.push(person);
  };

  TheatreSeatsConstructor.prototype.countOccupiedSeats =    function() {
    return priv.get(this).seats.length;
  };

  TheatreSeatsConstructor.prototype.isSoldOut = function() {
    return priv.get(this).seats.length >= this.maxSize;
  };

  TheatreSeatsConstructor.prototype.countFreeSeats = function() {
    return this.maxSize - priv.get(this).seats.length;
  };

  return  TheatreSeatsConstructor;

}());
```

As we can see, we no longer need the `id` property in order to identify the current object instance. We simply associate the current instance identified by the `this` keyword with the object containing the private members in the `priv` WeakMaps. Whenever we need to access our `seats` private member, we will refer to `priv.get(this).seats`.

The internal behavior of the WeakMap grants us a correct memory management since when an object instance is destroyed its private entry in the map will be removed by the garbage collector.

We can add a cosmetic touch to our code in order to make it less verbose by defining a custom function to access private members:

```
var  TheatreSeats = (function() {
  var priv = new WeakMap();
```

```
  var _= function(instance) {return priv.get(instance);};

function TheatreSeatsConstructor() {
  var privateMembers = {seats: []};

  priv.set(this, privateMembers);
  this.maxSize = 10;

}

TheatreSeatsConstructor.prototype.placePerson = function(person)    {
  _(this).seats.push(person);
};

TheatreSeatsConstructor.prototype.countOccupiedSeats =    function() {
  return _(this).seats.length;
};

TheatreSeatsConstructor.prototype.isSoldOut = function() {
  return _(this).seats.length >= this.maxSize;
};

TheatreSeatsConstructor.prototype.countFreeSeats = function() {
  return this.maxSize - _(this).seats.length;
};

  return  TheatreSeatsConstructor;

}());
```

This little change allows us to use a similar syntax when accessing public and private members. In the first case, we will use `this.publicMember`; in the second case, we will use `_(this).privateMember`, slightly recalling the convention-based approach syntax.

Property descriptors

Once we have found a satisfactory solution to control the visibility of an object's members, we have to face how public members can be accessed and which constraints we can set.

Controlling access to public properties

When we define public properties, we do not put any constraints on their accessibility. Consider the literal person definition:

```
var person = { name: "John", surname: "Smith"};
```

Public properties are readable and writable and they can be set to any value. The following assignments are perfectly legal:

```
var personName = person.name;

person.name = "Mario";
person.surname = [1, 2, 3];
```

But for the meaning we want to give to the object, these assignments might not make sense or not be desirable. Assigning an array to a person's surname is definitively bizarre!

In general, it would be desirable to have more control over the way to access public properties in order to determine as precisely as possible the meaning of an object. For example, consider the following definition of a person:

```
var person = {
  name: "John",
  surname: "Smith",
  fullName: "John Smith",
  email: "john.smith@packtpub.com"
};
```

We would like that the `fullName` property is read-only, and its value was calculated from the combination of the `name` and `surname` properties. Moreover, we would like to check that the `email` property was a syntactically valid e-mail address.

We can obtain this behavior using methods instead of properties, as shown in the following example:

```
var person = {
  name: "John",
  surname: "Smith",
  getFullName: function() { ... },
  getEmail: function() { ... },
  setEmail: function() { ... }
};
```

But it may be less intuitive and elegant and leads to designing all members as actions instead of distinguishing between data and actions, as reality abstraction would require. A better and natural approach should be based on properties, accessing their values using the same syntax.

Using getters and setters

Although often we are used to seeing objects with public properties without any access control, JavaScript allows us to accurately describe properties. In fact, we can use descriptors in order to control how a property can be accessed and which logic we can apply to it. Consider the following example:

```
var person = {
  name: "John",
  surname: "Smith",
  get fullName() { return this.name + " " + this.surname; },
  email: "john.smith@packtpub.com"
};
```

The `fullName` property is defined through a descriptor that allows us to define what is usually called a **getter**, which is a function returning a value for a property. Our getter returns the value of the `fullName` property as the concatenation of the `name` and `surname` properties. Although this definition of a person object seems quite similar to the one that uses a method returning the full name, it allows us to use the standard property syntax:

```
console.log(person.fullName); //John Smith
```

We can try to assign a value to the `fullName` property, but when we read it we will always get the concatenation of `name` and `surname` as the result:

```
person.fullName = "Mario Rossi";
```

```
console.log(person.fullName); //John Smith
```

Another type of descriptor is the **setter**, that is a function that sets a value for a property. For example, we could allow to set a value to the `fullName` property and split its value so that `name` and `surname` properties can be updated. We can use a convention to distinguish the name and surname by considering the first white space as a separator. The following is an example of implementation of a setter for the `fullName` property:

```
var person = {
  name: "John",
  surname: "Smith",
  get fullName() { return this.name + " " + this.surname; },
```

```
  set fullName(value) {
    var parts = value.toString().split(" ");
    this.name = parts[0] || "";
    this.surname = parts[1] || "";
  },
  email: "john.smith@packtpub.com"
};
```

Here, we defined a setter for `fullName` property by means of a function that takes an argument, `value`, splits it in to two parts based on a white space character, and assigns the first part to the `name` property and the second part to the `surname` property. This allows us to use the `fullName` property as in the following example:

```
console.log(person.fullName); //John Smith

person.fullName = "Mario Rossi";

console.log(person.name);      //Mario
console.log(person.surname);   //Rossi
console.log(person.fullName);  //Mario Rossi
```

As we can see, getters and setters allow us to create properties that do not act just as containers of values, but have an active role in the object's life.

Describing properties

In the preceding example, we declared a getter and a setter for the `fullName` property directly in the literal object. This is a quick and convenient way to get control over properties. However, not always, it is the best way to define properties with an advanced behavior.

Consider, for example, the definition of a constructor. How can we specify a getter or a setter in this case? We can use an alternative approach based on the `Object.defineProperty()` method. This method takes three arguments: the first argument is the object to add the property to, the second is the name of the property, and the third is the property's descriptor. For instance, we can define the constructor for our person object as follows:

```
var  Person = (function() {

  function PersonConstructor() {
    this.name = "";
    this.surname = "";
    this.email = "";
```

```
Object.defineProperty(
  this,
  "fullName",
  {
    get: function() { return this.name + " " +
    this.surname;},
    set: function(value) {
      var parts = value.toString().split(" ");
      this.name = parts[0] || "";
      this.surname = parts[1] || "";
    }
  });
}

return  PersonConstructor;

}());
```

As we can see, the `fullName` property is defined through the `Object.defineProperty()` method. The third parameter is the property descriptor that allows us to attach a getter and a setter to the property in a similar way as in the literal case. While in the previous case, the `get` and `set` keywords were sort of decorators of the methods, here they represents properties of the descriptor object.

At first glance, the definition of getters and setters inside a constructor does not add anything more to the `fullName` property than its definition inside a literal. We can use the property as in the previous examples. However, using `Object.defineProperty()` gives more control over our property definition. For example, we can specify if the property we are describing can be dynamically deleted or redefined, if its value can be changed, and so on. We can such constraints by setting the following properties of the descriptor object:

- **writable:** This is a Boolean that says whether the value of the property can be changed; its default value is *false*
- **configurable:** This is a Boolean that says whether the property's descriptor can be changed or the property itself can be deleted; its default value is *false*
- **enumerable:** This is a Boolean indicating whether the property can be accessed in a loop over the object's properties; its default value is *false*
- **value:** This represents the value associated to the property; its default value is *undefined*

As we can see, the default values of these constraints are very restrictive. For example, the following description of the `age` property does not explicitly define getters and setters:

```
Object.defineProperty(person, "age", { value: 28 })
```

We can access its value, but we cannot change it, since the default value of the `writable` constraint is *false*:

```
console.log(person.age);      //28
person.age = 22;
console.log(person.age);      //28
```

We have to pay attention when combining constraints in a property descriptor, since some combinations are not allowed. For example, if we define a `value` for a property, we cannot add a getter or a setter.

Moreover, it is very important to understand the difference between defining a property by assigning it a value and defining a property using `Object.defineProperty()`. The default constraints are very different. If we define a property by assigning a value, we will be able to change its value, to enumerate the property, and to redefine or delete it. In other words, suppose we create a property using the following code:

```
var person = {};

person.name = "John";
```

It corresponds to create the property as follows:

```
var person = {};

Object.defineProperty(
  person,
  "name",
  {
    value: "John",
    writable: true,
    configurable: true,
    enumerable: true
});
```

On the other hand, if we create a property using the `Object.defineProperty()` method, we put more restrictive constraints on its usage. This means that the following code:

```
var person = {};

Object.defineProperty(person, "name", { value: "John" });
```

Corresponds to the following explicit settings:

```
var person = {};

Object.defineProperty(
```

```
    person,
    "name",
    {
      value: "John",
      writable: false,
      configurable: false,
      enumerable: false
    });
```

Properties with internal state

In previous examples, we defined a `fullName` property whose value was based on existing public properties `name` and `surname`. Sometimes, we need to define a property whose value is not directly exposed, maybe because we need to make some processing on it before storing or returning it. In this case, we need a private variable where the actual value of the property is stored. Consider the example of an e-mail address of a person. We want that only a syntactically valid address can be assigned to an `email` property of our person object. In this case, we can add the property as in the following example:

```
var Person = (function() {

  function PersonConstructor() {
    var _email = "";

    this.name = "";
    this.surname = "";

    Object.defineProperty(
      this,
      "fullName",
      {
        get: function() { return this.name + " " + this.surname; },
        set: function(value) {
          var parts = value.toString().split(" ");

          this.name = parts[0] || "";
          this.surname = parts[1] || "";
        }
      });

    Object.defineProperty(
      this,
      "email",
      {
        get: function() { return _email; },
```

```
      set: function(value) {
        var emailRegExp = /\w+@\w+\.\w{2,4}/i;
        if (emailRegExp.test(value)) {
          _email = value;
        } else {
          throw new Error("Invalid email address!");
        }
      }
    });
  }

  return  PersonConstructor;

}());
```

In this example, we highlighted the code we added to support the new `email` property. As we can see, a private variable named _email has been declared inside the constructor, in order to store the internal state of the property. The `Object.defineProperty()` method is used to define a getter and a setter for the `email` property. In particular, the setter checks the validity of the passed value using a regular expression. If the value is not valid, an exception is thrown. We can verify this by executing the following code:

```
var p = new Person();

p.email = "john.smith";    //throws exception
```

The attempt to set a string that is not a syntactically valid e-mail address throws an exception as expected.

Since getters and setters are basically methods that control the access to properties and the internal state of a property is nothing but a private member, we have again to face the same problem seen while trying to hide private data. If we define a property inside the body of the constructor, we will replicate that code for each object instance. The best option should be to define getters and setters of our properties following the guidelines seen for information hiding.

Following these guidelines, we can redefine our `Person()` constructor as follows:

```
var Person = (function() {
  var priv = new WeakMap();
  var _= function(instance) {return priv.get(instance);};

  function PersonConstructor() {
    var privateMembers = { email: "" };

    priv.set(this, privateMembers);
```

```
    this.name = "";
    this.surname = "";
  }

  Object.defineProperty(
    PersonConstructor.prototype,
    "fullName",
    {
      get: function() { return this.name + " " + this.surname;}
    });

    Object.defineProperty(
      PersonConstructor.prototype,
      "email",
      {
        get: function() { return _(this).email; },
        set: function(value) {
          var emailRegExp = /\w+@\w+\.\w{2,4}/i;

          if (emailRegExp.test(value)) {
            _(this).email = value;
          } else {
            throw new Error("Invalid email address!");
          }
        }
      });

  return  PersonConstructor;

}());
```

We defined the internal state of the `email` property using the WeakMap approach and created the properties outside the `PersonConstructor()` function. Note that in this case, we attached the properties to the `PersonConstructor` function's prototype.

Information hiding in ES6 classes

Implementing the information hiding principle using the ES6 syntax enhancements is not so different. As we said when introducing them, ES6 classes are nothing more than a new syntactic approach to define constructors and methods for our objects. The major benefits include a more concise syntax and the application of the best practices in the internal implementation of object creation.

So, in order to correctly protect our private members, we need again to use an IIFE in order to exploit its closure and WeakMaps to store private members. The following is a definition of the `TheatreSeats` class with private members protection:

```
var  TheatreSeats = (function() {
  "use strict";
  var priv = new WeakMap();
  var _= function(instance) {return priv.get(instance);};

  class TheatreSeatsClass {
    constructor() {
      var privateMembers = {seats: []};

      priv.set(this, privateMembers);
      this.maxSize = 10;

    }

    placePerson(person) {
      _(this).seats.push(person);
    }

    countOccupiedSeats() {
      return _(this).seats.length;
    }

    isSoldOut() {
      return _(this).seats.length >= this.maxSize;
    }

    countFreeSeats() {
      return this.maxSize - _(this).seats.length;
    }
  }

  return  TheatreSeatsClass;

}());
```

This code is more compact than the one created without using the class syntax. However, the data protection approach remains the same.

We can get rid of the IIFE using the ES6 module syntax, but this will be the topic of a later chapter.

ES6 syntax allows us to define properties as well. All we need is to prepend the `get` and `set` keywords to a method in order to define a getter and a setter for that property. Let's redefine our `Person()` constructor using ES6 syntax:

```
var  Person = (function() {
  "use strict";
  var priv = new WeakMap();
  var _= function(instance) {return priv.get(instance);};

  class PersonClass {
    constructor() {
      var privateMembers = { email: "" };

      priv.set(this, privateMembers);

      this.name = "";
      this.surname = "";
    }

    get fullName() {
      return this.name + " " + this.surname;
    }

    get email() {
      return _(this).email;
    }

    set email(value) {
      var emailRegExp = /\w+@\w+\.\w{2,4}/i;

      if (emailRegExp.test(value)) {
        _(this).email = value;
      } else {
        throw new Error("Invalid email address!");
      }
    }
  }

  return  PersonClass;

}());
```

Again, the new syntax is more compact and readable. This should be a strong reason to use ES6 syntax as soon as possible in our projects. Properties defined in classes are added as prototype methods so that they are shared with all object instances. However, currently we cannot control other constraints on a property like we made with the `Object.defineProperty()` method. Class properties are writable, configurable, but not enumerable by default.

Summary

In this chapter, we explored how JavaScript allows us to implement encapsulation and information hiding principles. We used an incremental approach that allows us to analyze the various techniques currently adopted by most developers to protect the private members of an object. We started by analyzing a very simple technique based on a property naming convention and showed its benefits and drawbacks. Then, we described the privacy levels approach and then defined a better approach that uses WeakMaps.

Along this walk-through, we introduced a couple of useful concepts and our solutions were based on closures and **Immediate Invoked Function Expressions (IIFE)**.

In addition to private member protection, we explored how to control access to public properties using getters, setters, and property descriptors.

At the end of the chapter, we explored how everything we discussed adapts to the new ECMAScript class syntax.

In the next chapter, we will see in detail how inheritance in JavaScript works and how we can create new objects by combining existing ones.

4
Inheriting and Creating Mixins

This chapter will deepen the prototypal inheritance of JavaScript, highlighting the difference with classical inheritance. It will also cover most of common patterns to implement overriding, member protection, and extension prevention. Multiple inheritance and mixins are also discussed always taking into account the new ECMAScript 6 syntax and features.

The following topics are covered in the chapter:

- Prototypal inheritance
- Overriding methods and properties
- Implementing protected members
- Controlling object extension
- Multiple inheritance and mixins

Why inheritance?

Inheritance is one of the fundamentals principle in Object-Oriented Programming. It is usually defined as a *is-a* relationship between objects (or classes, if the language supports them).

Consider, for example, a generic person and a student. We can say that the student **is a** person that is a student inherits all features of a generic person, but he has a specialized profile—he studies. This is true for other specialized profiles such as a teacher, a lawyer, a singer, and so on.

The *is-a* relationship keyword, and thus inheritance, informally says that if an object A inherits from object B, then we say that A is B, that is, A is a specialized version of B. Sometimes, A is also said to be a derived object of B, while B is usually called the base object or parent object.

But, why do we need inheritance in Object-Oriented Programming? Since a derived object has all the features of the base object, inheritance can help to reduce code redundancy between similar objects by sharing common features. In other words, a base object contains the common features and shares them with its derived objects. This also allows us to create more maintainable code, since we can change a feature just on the base object and share it instantly with all derived objects.

Objects and prototypes

Until now, we have seen two ways to create objects in JavaScript. The first and simplest approach is based on the literal notation:

```
var person = {name: "John", surname: "Smith"};
```

The second and more flexible approach is based on a constructor function:

```
function Person(name, surname) {
  this.name = name;
  this.surname = surname;
}

var person = new Person("John", "Smith");
```

There is no difference between the resulting objects of both approaches. Our feeling in both cases is that we have created two new objects from scratch. Actually, it is not true. In both cases, we created a derived object—an object derived from an instance of the built-in `Object()` constructor. It is a constructor that allows us to create a base object of all JavaScript objects—the empty object `{}`. Every object created using the literal notation or a constructor inherits all properties and methods of an instance of the empty object.

We can verify it by trying to call the `toString()` method:

```
var person = {name: "John", surname: "Smith"};

person.toString();    //result: "[object Object]"
```

We have not defined the `toString()` method; however, any object created using literal notation or a constructor function will have attached this method and some others inherited from the empty object. Moreover, even if we created an object using the literal notation, it also has a constructor associated. We can verify this using the inherited `constructor` property:

```
person.constructor.name;    //result: "Object"
```

We also can check that our object is an instance of the `Object` constructor using the `instanceof` operator:

```
console.log(person instanceof Object);   //result: true
```

All these tools confirm that the ways we know until now to create objects do not create objects from scratch, but create objects derived from an empty instance of the `Object()` constructor.

In JavaScript terminology, we say that the empty object is the **prototype** of our objects.

What is a prototype?

A prototype is an object that acts as a template for another object. We have no classes in JavaScript, so features are shared between objects through other objects taken as reference. In other words, if we need an object that is similar to an existing object A, we create a new object B saying that its prototype is the existing object A. This is the basic mechanism of JavaScript's inheritance.

All objects in JavaScript have a prototype, including functions. When we create an object using the literal notation, the prototype of the new object is the empty object `{ }`. When we create an object using a constructor function, the prototype of the new object is the prototype of the constructor function.

We can access the prototype of an object in two ways.

The first way is using the `prototype` property of its constructor. For example, if we have an object created using the `Person()` constructor, we can put the prototype of the object in a variable as follows:

```
var prototypeOfperson = person.constructor.prototype;
```

This approach is also valid for objects created with the literal notation, since they have a constructor function as well, the `Object()` constructor.

The second way to access an object's prototype is using the `Object.getPrototypeOf()` method, as shown here:

```
var prototypeOfperson = Object.getPrototypeOf(person);
```

In both approaches we get the object that acts as the template of the `person` object.

 A popular way to access an object's prototype uses the `__proto__` pseudo-property. This property was originally born as an internal property supported by some JavaScript engines in the browser environment to link an object to its prototype. Given its widespread support, ECMAScript 6 specifications standardized it, but added the `__proto__` property to the standard as a deprecated feature, to be used just for compatibility with legacy code.

We can check if an object is the prototype of another object using the `isPrototypeOf()` method owned by every object:

```
var p = Object.getPrototypeOf(person);

console.log(p.isPrototypeOf(person));    //result: true
console.log(person.isPrototypeOf(p));    //result: false
```

From this example, we can see that the prototype relation between objects is not a symmetric relation; that is, if object A is the prototype of object B, object B cannot be the prototype of object A.

Creating objects

The discussion concerning objects and prototypes bring us to affirm that object creation and inheritance are strictly connected. The two ways to create objects in JavaScript that we have seen, using literal notation and via a constructor function, generate objects with a built-in prototype. So, we have two questions:

- Can we create objects without a prototype?
- Can we create object with a specific prototype?

The answer to both questions is affirmative and the solution is the `Object.create()` method. This method allows us to create JavaScript objects using a functional approach and giving us more flexibility.

The `Object.create()` method was proposed by Douglas Crockford as a true functional alternative to using the `new` keyword and constructors, considered by him as not coherent with the nature of JavaScript.

We can create an object without a prototype in the following way:

```
var myObject = Object.create(null);
```

In this case, the `myObject` variable will contain an object without a prototype. It will not inherit the empty object features, so it will not have `toString()` and other standard methods we have seen earlier. If we try to check what the prototype of the object is, we will obtain the following:

```
console.log(Object.getPrototypeOf(myObject));     //result: null
```

The prototype of the object is `null`. Just the value we passed to the `Object.create()` method. In order to create an object whose prototype is another object we can specify it as the argument of `Object.create()`, as shown below:

```
var person = { name: "John", surname: "Smith"};

var myObject = Object.create(person);
```

Now `myObject` will have the `person` object as its prototype.

When creating an object with the `Object.create()` method, we can specify new properties for the new object. These properties can be specified as the second optional parameter of the `Object.create()` method, as shown in the following example:

```
var person = { name: "", surname: ""};
var developer = Object.create(
        person,
        { knownLanguage:
          {   writable: true,
            configurable: true
          }
        });
```

Here, we added the `knownLanguage` property to the `developer` object by specifying a property descriptor. As result, the developer object will have the properties inherited from its prototype object and the new property defined at the creation stage.

In addition to associating a prototype during the creation of an object with the `Object.create()` method, we can also assign a prototype to an object after the object is created. We can make this by using the `Object.setPrototypeOf()` method defined by ECMAScript 6 specifications. The following is an example of how we can use this method:

```
var person = {name: "John", surname: "Smith" };
var developer = { knownLanguage: "JavaScript" };

Object.setPrototypeOf(developer, person);
```

In this way, we assigned the `person` object as the prototype of the `developer` object. This instantly causes the `developer` object to inherit the `person`'s members `name` and `surname`:

```
console.log(developer.name);       //result: "John"
console.log(developer.surname);    //result: "Smith"
```

This is a sort of object combination executed at runtime. In fact, the `Object.setPrototypeOf()` method allows us to change at runtime the prototype of an object, modifying its features. In our example, the initial prototype of both `person` and `developer` objects was the empty object {}. After applying the `Object.setPrototypeOf()` method, the `developer` prototype has changed.

Although the `Object.setPrototypeOf()` method offers interesting possibilities, it should be pointed out that its use can have negative performance impacts due to dynamically linking the prototype at runtime. Using `Object.create()` allows JavaScript engines to statically analyze and optimize the code, while changing prototypes at runtime can have unpredictable effects on the performance.

Prototype chaining

When creating an object, we have the opportunity to specify its prototype thanks to the `Object.create()` method. This allows the new object to inherit features of the prototype. Being a regular object, a prototype in turn has its own prototype. Consider, for example, the following code:

```
var person = { name: "John", surname: "Smith"};
var developer = Object.create(
        person,
        { knownLanguage:
          {   writable: true,
            configurable: true
          }
        });
```

When using the `developer` object, we can access the `knownLanguage` property, as it was added during the object's creation, and the `name` and `surname` properties, as they are inherited from its prototype, the `person` object. However, the `person` object has its own prototype. Since it has been created using the literal notation, its prototype is the empty object {}. So, the `person` object inherits the standard object's members, such as the `toString()` method. We can simply verify that also the `developer` object inherits the `toString()` method:

```
console.log(developer.toString());    //result: "[object Object]"
```

This shows that inheritance is a relationship among many objects, not just between two objects. An object inherits all members of its prototype and the ones of the prototype's prototype, and so on. The sequence of links between objects through the prototype relationship is usually called `prototype chain`.

But, what does inheriting members from the prototype mean exactly?

The inheritance mechanism is extremely simple. When we try to access an object's member, the system searches first among the object's members. If the member is not found, the system searches among the members of the object's prototype. If again it is not found, the system goes up the prototype chain until it finds the searched member or it finds a null value. In the first case, the found member's value is returned; otherwise, an `undefined` value is returned. The following picture shows how JavaScript goes up the prototype chain in order to access the `toString()` method in our previous example:

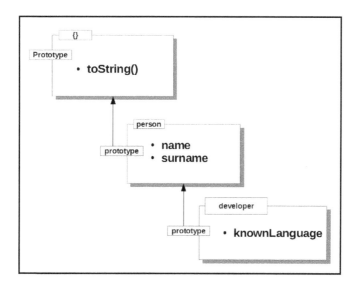

The way JavaScript looks for an object's members in the prototype chain should make us think about the effects on performance when the chain is too long. In fact, while this mechanism give us a great flexibility and low memory consumption, it has a performance cost. So, we should limit the prototype chain in order to reduce performance issues in our JavaScript applications.

Inheritance and constructors

Although basic inheritance in JavaScript is a relationship between objects, we would like to manage it while using object constructors. In other words, we want to have a way that allow us to create objects through a constructor function that inherits features from other objects. This actually would define an inheritance relationship between constructors.

Let's consider the constructor for person objects:

```
function Person(name, surname) {
  this.name = name;
  this.surname =  surname;
}
```

We would like to define a constructor for developer objects that inherit features from objects created by the Person() constructor. The following code achieves this goal:

```
function Developer(name, surname, knownLanguage) {
  Person.apply(this, arguments);
  this.knownLanguage =  knownLanguage;
}
```

The main difference between a standard constructor is the use of method apply() of the Person() constructor. The apply() method executes the Person() function by taking the Developer context and arguments. The final effect is the creation of the Person function's properties on the Developer instance.

When we create an instance of Developer, we will get an object with name, surname and knownLanguage properties:

```
var johnSmith = new Developer("John", "Smith", "JavaScript");

console.log(johnSmith.name);               //result:  "John"
console.log(johnSmith.surname);            //result:  "Smith"
console.log(johnSmith.knownLanguage );  //result:  "JavaScript"
```

This approach let's us inherit `Person`'s members into `Developer` objects. However, it breaks the consistency of the `instanceof` operator on the prototype chain. Let's explain with the following example:

```
var johnSmith = new Developer("John", "Smith", "JavaScript");

johnSmith instanceof Developer;    //result:  true
johnSmith instanceof Person;       //result:  false
johnSmith instanceof Object;       //result:  true
```

Here, we can see that the instance of `Developer` is not also considered also an instance of `Person`. We should fix this issue by explicitly assign a prototype the `Developer()` constructor:

```
Developer.prototype = Object.create(Person.prototype);
Developer.prototype.constructor = Developer;
```

ES6 inheritance

The `class` construct introduced by the ECMAScript 6 specifications also brings a new way to define inheritance. Using a syntax similar to most common classical Object-Oriented Programming languages, we can make a class inherit from another one. Let's take the previous example of person and developer and rewrite it using classes:

```
class Person {
  constructor(name, surname) {
    this.name = name;
    this.surname = surname;
  }
}


class Developer extends Person {
  constructor(name, surname, knownLanguage) {
    super(name, surname);
    this. knownLanguage = knownLanguage;
  }
}
```

In this example, we have highlighted the relevant parts of inheritance. As we can see, the class `Developer` inherits from the class `Person` using the `extends` keyword. Moreover, in its constructor the `Developer` class calls its parent class using the `super` keyword. This code is a more compact and readable way to get the same functionalities using the following constructor functions:

```
function Person(name, surname) {
  this.name = name;
  this.surname = surname;
}

function Developer(name, surname, knownLanguage) {
  Person.apply(this, arguments);
  this.knownLanguage =  knownLanguage;
}


Developer.prototype = Object.create(Person.prototype);
Developer.prototype.constructor = Developer;
```

The `super` keyword can be used in two ways:

- In a class constructor method, to call the parent constructor
- Inside a method of a class, to use methods of the parent class

In the first case, we can use it as a function passing any parameters, as we saw in the `Developer` class definition. In the second case, we can use it as an object that exposes methods, as in the following example:

```
class Person {
  constructor(name, surname) {
    this.name = name;
    this.surname = surname;
  }

  getFullName() {
    return this.name + " " + this.surname;
  }
}


class Developer extends Person {
  constructor(name, surname, knownLanguage) {
    super(name, surname);
    this. knownLanguage = knownLanguage;
  }
```

```
  displayCompetency() {
    console.log(super.getFullName() + " knows " +
    this.knownLanguage);
  }
}
```

Classes and traditional constructor functions can coexist in an application. For example, it is possible to define a class that inherits from a constructor function, as shown in the following code:

```
function Person(name, surname) {
  this.name = name;
  this.surname = surname;
}

class Developer extends Person {
  constructor(name, surname, knownLanguage) {
    super(name, surname);
    this.knownLanguage = knownLanguage;
  }
}
```

However, it is not possible to do the opposite, that is, define a constructor function that inherits from a class.

Controlling inheritance

Inheritance of members between objects is a powerful feature. However, in some situation, we want to control how member are passed from the parent object to the child and what a derived object can do with inherited members. Let's analyze the most common ways to control inheritance in JavaScript.

Overriding methods

When creating a derived object, we usually want to give it a slightly different behavior from parent object. This new behavior can be implemented by adding new methods or properties, but sometimes we need to redefine a method or a property of the parent object. In this case, we are talking about **overriding**.

Let's consider an example of a `Person` definition with a `getFullName()` method returning the concatenation of `name` and `surname`:

```
function Person(name, surname) {
  this.name = name;
  this.surname = surname;
}

Person.prototype.getFullName = function() {
  return this.name + " " + this.surname;
}
```

Now, we want `Developer` inheriting from `Person`, but the `getFullName()` method should display the `Dev` prefix as title, as in `Dev John Smith`. We could create a new method, such as `getDevFullName()`, but it would be not intuitive and redundant. Instead, we can override the `getFullName()` method as shown in the following example:

```
function Developer(name, surname, knownLanguage) {
  Person.apply(this, arguments);
  this.knownLanguage =  knownLanguage;
}

Developer.prototype = new Person();
Developer.prototype.constructor = Developer;
Developer.prototype.getFullName = function() {
  return "Dev " + Person.prototype.getFullName.call(this); };
```

The highlighted code shows how to override the `getFullName()` method of the `Person()` constructor. We attach to the `Developer` prototype property a method with the same name. In this case, the overriding method internally uses the parent's method, so we have to pay attention to the way we call it. Since, we want that the method refers to the current `Developer` instance and not to the `Person` instance, we invoke the `Person`'s `getFullName()` method using the `call()` method and passing the `this` keyword. This way ensure us that the `Person` function's `getFullName()` method will act on the `Developer` instance's `name` and `surname` properties.

 Any JavaScript function has the `call()` and `apply()` methods. Both run the function in the context of the first argument, but while `call()` accepts a list of values as the function's parameters, `apply()` accepts an array of values.

So, when we use the `Person` function's `getFullName()` method, we will obtain the concatenation of `name` and `surname` properties. When we use the `Developer` instance's `getFullName()` method, we will get the same result preceded by the title `Dev`:

```
var johnSmith = new Person("John", "Smith");
var marioRossi = new Developer("Mario", "Rossi", "JavaScript");

console.log(johnSmith.getFullName());      //result: "John Smith"
console.log(marioRossi.getFullName());     //result: "Dev Mario  Rossi"
```

As we would expect, the new ECMAScript 6 syntax allows us to simplify the way we can override a method. In fact, we can simply redefine the overriding method in our derived class and, if necessary, call the parent class using the `super` keyword. The following example shows how we can override the `Person` function's `getFullName()` method obtaining the same result seen earlier:

```
class Developer extends Person {
  constructor(name, surname, knownLanguage) {
    super(name, surname);
    this. knownLanguage = knownLanguage;
  }

  getFullName() {
    return "Dev "+  super.getFullName();
  }
}
```

Overriding properties

Property overriding is a common operation in JavaScript. Every time we define a constructor that inherits from some other constructor, we are overriding the parent's properties. Let's consider again the `Developer` constructor definition:

```
function Developer(name, surname, knownLanguage) {
  Person.apply(this, arguments);
  this.knownLanguage =  knownLanguage;
}

Developer.prototype = new Person();
Developer.prototype.constructor = Developer;
```

When we call the `Person` constructor through the `apply()` method, we are asking the parent object to replicate its properties on the `Developer` instance, identified by the `this` keyword. So, the `Developer` instance's `name` and `surname` properties are overriding the `Person` function's properties.

This makes sense, since we usually do not want to share properties with the parent. Each instance usually should have its own properties. So, the simplest way to override a parent property is redefine it in the child constructor.

However, there are situations where a property can be conveniently shared among all instances of an object constructor and all object children. By referring to our `Person` constructor, when we want to have a `fullName` property whose value is dependent on the `name` and `surname` properties. We are talking about implementing the `getFullName()` method functionality as a property. We can do it as follows:

```
function Person(name, surname) {
  this.name = name;
  this.surname = surname;
}

Object.defineProperty(
          Person.prototype,
          "fullName", {
            get: function() { return this.name + " " +
            this.surname; }
          });
```

Here we define a read-only property using `Object.defineProperty()` and attaching it to the `Person` function's prototype. The `fullName` property will be available to any instance and will be inherited by derived constructors.

If we want to change the `fullName` property behavior in the `Developer` constructor so that it attaches the `Dev` title, we can proceed as in the following example:

```
Object.defineProperty(
          Developer.prototype,
          "fullName", {
            get: function() { return "Dev " + this.name + " " +
            this.surname; }
          });
```

As we can see, we simply redefined the property using `Object.defineProperty()`. Here, we attached the `fullName` property to the `Developer`prototype and changed the output of the `get` descriptor.

This allows us to have different values of the `fullName` property depending on the object's prototype:

```
var johnSmith = new Person("John", "Smith");
var marioRossi = new Developer("Mario", "Rossi", "JavaScript");

console.log(johnSmith.fullName);      //result: "John Smith"
console.log(marioRossi.fullName);     //result: "Dev Mario Rossi"
```

Protected members

In the previous chapter, we talked about object members, visibility and accessibility. Following Crockford, we classified them in public, private, and privileged. Most of the classical OOP languages provide another category of members that involves inheritance: **protected** members. In general, a protected member is a private member only visible to derived objects. It represents a privacy level that stays between the public and the private: a sort of privacy shared among objects involved in a common inheritance.

Once again, JavaScript does not does built-in support for protected members, so we need to implement it ourselves. A common pattern to emulate the support of protected members is to ask them expressly to the parent object constructor. Let's explain with an example.

Suppose that our `Person()` constructor has a private utility function that capitalizes the first letter of the values of the `name` and `surname` properties:

```
var Person = (function() {
  function capitalize(string) {
    return string.charAt(0).toUpperCase() + string.slice(1);
  }

  function PersonConstructor(name, surname) {
    this.name = capitalize(name);
    this.surname = capitalize(surname);
  }

  return PersonConstructor;
}());
```

The `capitalize()` function is implemented as a private member and it is not publicly accessible. It allows us to pass a name and surname to the constructor without worry about upper or lower case:

```
var p = new Person("john", "smith");

console.log(p.name);     //result: "John"
```

If we want to make this function available to all derived objects, that is, to make it protected, we can implement it as follows:

```
var Person = (function() {
  var protectedMembers;

  function capitalize(string) {
    return string.charAt(0).toUpperCase() + string.slice(1);
  }

  function PersonConstructor(name, surname, protected) {
    protectedMembers = protected || {};
    protectedMembers.capitalize = capitalize;

    this.name = capitalize(name);
    this.surname = capitalize(surname);
  }

  return PersonConstructor;
}());
```

The highlighted code shows that we have defined a private variable named `protectedMembers`. We also added a new parameter to the internal constructor, named `protected`. This parameter is the means that allows the derived constructor to ask the parent constructor for the protected members. Inside the `PersonConstructor()` function, we ensure that the `protected` parameter is not empty and add to it the `capitalize()` method.

Now, we define the `Developer` constructor so that it asks its parent constructor for protected members:

```
function Developer(name, surname, knownLanguage) {
  var parentProtected = {};
  Person.call(this, name, surname, parentProtected);

  this.knownLanguage = parentProtected.capitalize(knownLanguage);
}
```

Since the private variable `parentProtected` is an object, it is passed by reference to the `Person()` function. So, the changes made by the parent constructor to the `parentProtected` variable are available inside the `Developer()` constructor. This allow us to use the `capitalize()` function attached to `parentProtected` object.

Preventing extensions

We don't always want derived constructors or classes to customize some or all members of the parent constructor or class. In some circumstances, we want to prevent that certain changes being allowed. In the previous chapter, we have seen how to prevent that a property is written or its configuration changed. But what can we do to prevent property or method addition and removal? Luckily, we have `Object.preventExtensions()`, `Object.seal()`, and `Object.freeze()` methods that help us.

Let's begin to see in which situations we can use these methods.

If we want to prevent addition of new members to an object we can use the `Object.preventExtensions()` method. Consider the following example:

```
var person = { name: "John", surname: "Smith"};

Object.preventExtensions(person);

person.age = 32;

console.log(person.age);    //result: undefined
```

If we try to add the new property, `age`, to the `person` object, we do not get an error, but the property will not be added to it. If we enable strict mode, the attempt to add the new property will throw an exception. In order to avoid to raise the exception, we should check if the object is extensible using the `Object.isExtensible()` method:

```
if (Object.isExtensible(person)) {
  person.age = 32;
}
```

Of course, we can use the `Object.preventExtensions()` method in a constructor in order to avoid property addition both to the constructor instances and the derived constructors. For example, we can define the `Person()` constructor as follows:

```
function Person(name, surname) {
  this.name = name;
  this.surname = surname;

  Object.preventExtensions(this);
}
```

With this definition, any derived constructor will not be able to add new properties:

```
function Developer(name, surname, knownLanguage) {
  Person.apply(this, arguments);
  this.knownLanguage =  knownLanguage;
}
```

If we create an instance of `Developer`, we will find that it has not the `knownLanguage` property, even if it is added in the constructor:

```
var dev = new Developer("Mario", "Rossi", "JavaScript");
console.log(dev.knownLanguage);    //result:    undefined
```

Although `Object.preventExtensions()` prevent members addition, we can still remove them using the `delete` statement and change property configuration using `Object.defineProperty()`. If we also need to prevent these changes, we have to use the `Object.seal()` method:

```
function Person(name, surname) {
  this.name = name;
  this.surname = surname;

  Object.seal(this);
}
```

Now, any attempt to delete a member or change the configuration of a property will fail:

```
var person = new Person("John", "Smith");

console.log(delete person.name);    //result:    false
console.log(person.name);           //result:    "John"
```

Of course, we still will not be able to add new members to the object.

We can check if an object is sealed using the `Object.isSealed()` method:

```
if (!Object.isSealed(person)) {
  delete person.name;
}
```

Even if we cannot add or remove members to a sealed object nor modify their configuration, we can still change its members value.

If necessary, we can make an object immutable using the `Object.freeze()` method. This is an extreme measure when we want that the structure of an object will not change and its members should be read-only:

```
var person = new Person("John", "Smith");

Object.freeze(person);

person.age = 32;
console.log(person.age);      //result: undefined

person.name = "Mario";
console.log(person.name);     //result: "John"

delete person.name;           //result:   false
console.log(person.name);     //result: "John"

Object.defineProperty(
    person,
    "name",
    { get: function() { return "Mario"; }
    });
                         //result: exception
```

We can check if an object is immutable using the `Object.isFrozen()` method:

```
if (!Object.isFrozen(person)) {
  person.name = "Mario";
}
```

Implementing multiple inheritance

The prototypal mechanism of inheritance leads us to the conclusion that JavaScript supports single inheritance. In fact, since an object has just one prototype link and we can assign just one prototype object to a constructor function, we can conclude that an object can inherit features from just one other object. However, the flexibility of JavaScript allow us to implement multiple inheritance in a simple way.

But what is multiple inheritance? It is the ability to inherit features from more than one object or class at the same time. Suppose, for example, that we have two constructors or classes: Developer and Student. We want to be able to create objects that represent developers who study, that is, objects that inherit features both from the Developer and Student. Multiple inheritance allows us to compose features deriving from more than one object or class into a new type of object. Let's explain how to implement it in JavaScript.

We start from our Developer() and Student() constructors, as shown by the following code:

```
function Developer(name, surname, knownLanguage) {
  Person.apply(this, arguments);
  this.knownLanguage =  knownLanguage;
}

function Student(name, surname, subjectOfStudy) {
  Person.apply(this, arguments);
  this.subjectOfStudy =  subjectOfStudy;
}
```

Both constructors inherit from the Person() constructor seen in previous pages, but it is not relevant to our reasoning. The following constructor function will create objects that share features from Developer and Student objects:

```
function DevStudent(name, surname, knownLanguage, subjectOfStudy) {
  Developer.call(this, name, surname, knownLanguage);
  Student.call(this, name, surname, subjectOfStudy);
}
```

We have simply invoked the constructors we inherit using the call() method. This allows us to get objects that have name, surname, knownLanguage, and subjectOfStudy properties, as shown here:

```
var johnSmith = new DevStudent("John", "Smith", "C#",  "JavaScript");

console.log(johnSmith.knownLanguage);     //result: C#
console.log(johnSmith.subjectOfStudy);    //result: JavaScript
```

This way to implement multiple inheritance is pretty simple, but may have some issues. What happens if two parent constructors have a member with the same name? We actually had such issues in our example, but we do not worried about it. In fact, both `Developer()` and `Student()` constructors provide `name` and `surname` properties. When we invoked the parent constructors in `DevStudent()` function, the `Student()` constructor redefined `name` and `surname` derived from `Developer()` constructor. Since they have the same meaning, we have no side effect. But what happens if there is a name collision on members that have different meaning or behavior? If no action is taken, the last parent constructor will override any previous definition. So, the order of parent constructors calls matters when implementing multiple inheritance.

While implementing multiple inheritance is so simple with constructor functions, it is not the same when we want to use the `class` construct of ECMAScript 6. The `extends` keyword does not allow to specify more than one class, so we cannot have a definition like the following:

```
class DevStudent extends Developer, Student {
  ...
}
```

However, since the right-hand side of the `extends` clause can be any expression, we can make classes inherit from more than one class by exploiting the **mixin** pattern.

Creating and using mixins

The term **mixin** is usually used to specify a collection of functions available to be shared among objects or classes. It can be somehow considered similar to abstract classes in classical OOP languages. Usually, the mixin functions are not directly used, but they are *borrowed* to others objects or classes in order to extend them without creating a strict relationship as it could be with inheritance. Let's introduce mixins in JavaScript with a simple example.

Mixing prototypes

Consider our `Person()` constructor function in its minimal implementation:

```
function Person(name, surname) {
  this.name = name;
  this.surname = surname;
}
```

Then consider a simple object literal implementing a `getFullName()` method that returns the full name based on the existing `name` and `surname` properties:

```
var myMixin = {
  getFullName: function() {
    return this.name + " " + this.surname;
  }
};
```

This object is our mixin. It implements a generic function, not bound to a specific object constructor and available to be *mixed* with the members of other objects. In order to enable the mixing of the members, we need a specific function such as the following:

```
function augment(destination, source) {
  for (var methodName in source) {
    if (source.hasOwnProperty(methodName)) {
      destination[methodName] = source[methodName];
    }
  }
  return destination;
}
```

The goal of this function is to add (or replace) methods of the object passed as second argument to the object represented by the first argument. Often such function is named *extend*, but we prefer to call it *augment* in order to avoid confusion with inheritance extension.

ECMAScript 6 introduced the method `Object.assign()` that has exactly the same behavior of our an `augment()` function. So, we may actually replace each occurrence of an `augment()` invocation with `Object.assign()`.

With this tool, we can easily add the members of our mixin to the members created by the `Person()` constructor:

```
augment(Person.prototype, myMixin);
```

Now, when we will create a `Person` instance, it will include the `getFullName()` method taken from the mixin:

```
var johnSmith = new Person("John", "Smith");

console.log(johnSmith.getFullName());    //result: "John Smith"
```

Of course, we can add methods from different mixins and compose the public interface of our objects as needed. For example, assuming that we have different mixins collecting functionalities grouped by topic, we can mix members with the following code:

```
augment(Person.prototype, namingMixin);
augment(Person.prototype, movingMixin);
augment(Person.prototype, studyingMixin);
```

Here, we add to the `Person()` prototype from a mixin that provides utilities concerning name and surname management (`namingMixin`), a mixin with methods describing movement (`movingMixin`), and a mixin that has methods regarding study activities (`studyingMixin`).

A more accurate mixin function might allow us to select which members to add:

```
function augment(destination, source, ...methodNames) {
  if (methodNames) {
    for (var methodName of methodNames) {
      if (source.hasOwnProperty(methodName)) {
        destination[methodName] = source[methodName];
      }
    }
  } else {
    for (var methodName in source) {
      if (source.hasOwnProperty(methodName)) {
        destination[methodName] = source[methodName];
      }
    }
  }

  return destination;
}
```

In this case, we added the rest parameter `methodNames` to allow an indefinite number of parameters after the source and destination ones. If a list of method names is passed, the function adds just them to the destination object. This allows us to select members to add from a mixin, as in the following example:

```
augment(Person.prototype, namingMixin, "getFullName");
augment(Person.prototype, movingMixin, "goLeft", "goRight");
augment(Person.prototype, studyingMixin, "readTopic", "writeTopic",
"repeatTopic");
```

Mixing classes

We can apply the mixin pattern based on prototype augmentation to classes as well. Let's consider, for example, the `Person` class definition:

```
class Person {
  constructor(name, surname) {
    this.name = name;
    this.surname = surname;
  }
}
```

Since classes are equivalent to standard constructor functions, they can be extended with the `augment()` function or the `Object.assign()` method, as shown by the following code:

```
augment(Person.prototype, myMixin);
```

As for the constructors case, we can create a `Person` instance with the `getFullName()` method:

```
var johnSmith = new Person("John", "Smith");

console.log(johnSmith.getFullName());    //result: "John Smith"
```

Although this approach is fully functional, a more consistent approach should be integrated with class syntax. To achieve this goal, we define a function that extends a generic class with our mixin:

```
function mixNamingWith(superclass) {
  return class extends superclass {
    getFullName() {
      return this.name + " " + this.surname;
    }
  }
}
```

This function takes a class as argument and returns a subclass extended with our `getFullName()` method. This allows us to define a new class that includes methods from the mixin, as follows:

```
class ExtendedPerson extends mixNamingWith(Person) { }

var johnSmith = new ExtendedPerson("John", "Smith");

console.log(johnSmith .getFullName());    //result: "John Smith"
```

If we need to compose a class from many mixin, we can make nested calls to mixin functions as shown here:

```
class ExtendedPerson extends
      mixNamingWith(
        mixMovingWith(
          mixStudyingWith(
            Person
          )
        )
      ) { }
```

Summary

In this chapter, we explored the inheritance mechanism of JavaScript based on prototypes, which is objects that act as templates for other objects. We saw how objects can be linked each other through their prototypes to create a chain representing the inheritance hierarchy. Then, we talked about the creation of an inheritance relationship between constructor functions and about the simplicity of new ECMAScript 6 syntax for extending classes. Our discussion continued with the different ways to control inheritance: from overriding methods and properties to the implementation of protected members, from the prevention of object extension to the creation of immutable objects.

The chapter concluded with some examples of implementation of multiple inheritance and with the use of the mixin pattern with constructor functions and classes.

The next chapter will discuss interoperability between objects. We will see how we can define contracts, how to specify them through interfaces, and how to use duck typing.

5
Defining Contracts with Duck Typing

This chapter will illustrate an enhanced technique that allows us to define contracts between objects interacting each other. This technique, named **duck typing**, allows for implementing something similar to interfaces supported by many classical Object-Oriented Programming languages. The topics covered by the chapter are:

- Checking dynamic data types
- Contracts between software components
- Using duck typing
- Emulating interfaces with duck typing

Managing dynamic typing

Data types are one of the basic features that ensure consistency throughout an application. Some operations can be made only on specific data types and checking if a value is of a valid data type is crucial to avoid runtime exceptions. Most compiled Object-Oriented Programming languages have a static type system that asks the developer to declare the allowed type of a variable and check the code before it runs. JavaScript is a dynamic language—it does not require you to declare a specific data type for a variable. Since the content of a variable can change during the execution, data type checking of its value is performed just when the value itself is used. Let's recall some basic notions with some examples.

Dynamic data types

We know that a variable does not have an associated type declaration in JavaScript. It can contain any value and its type depends on its content. This does not mean that JavaScript does not support data types. It just means that a variable is not constrained to support a certain type of value.

Let's consider the following function definition:

```
function square(n) {
  return n * n;
}
```

In the intention of the developer, it calculates the square of a number. In fact, if we pass a number to this function we will get the correct output value:

```
console.log(square(3));          //result: 9
```

But, what happens if we pass a value other than a number, say a string? JavaScript is very tolerant and it tries to return a value by making some implicit type conversions. For example, if we pass a string representing a number we will get again the correct output value:

```
console.log(square("3"));          //result: 9
```

But if we pass different string values or different data type values, we will get results that do not resemble square numbers, as maybe the developer wanted:

```
console.log(square("three"));     //result: NaN
console.log(square(true));        //result: 1
console.log(square({a: 2}));      //result: NaN
```

If we want that a function accepts only a specific data type, we have to check it ourselves, as follows:

```
function square(n) {
  var result;

  if (typeof n === "number") {
    result = n*n;
  } else {
    throw new Error("Wrong data type!")
  }

  return result;
}
```

This generates an exception when we try to execute it on a value that is not a number:

```
console.log(square("three"));    //result: Error: Wrong data type!
```

Data typing and objects

We can easily check primitive data types by using the `typeof` operator. But can we use it for objects? Let's consider a constructor that represents a software house:

```
function SoftwareHouse() {
  this.employees = [];

}

SoftwareHouse.prototype.hire = function(dev) {
  this.employees.push(dev);
};
```

As we know, we can also define it using the ECMAScript 6 `class` construct:

```
class SoftwareHouse {
  constructor() {
    this.employees = [];
  }

  hire(dev) {
    this.employees.push(dev);
  }
}
```

Regardless of the syntax used, we defined a constructor of objects that has a list of employees and a method that hires developers.

The `hire()` method does no checking on the values passed. This seems unlikely, since the software house would hire just persons, not every type of object:

```
var johnSmith = {name: "John", surname: "Smith"};
var lassie = {name: "Lassie", breed: "Collie"};
var table = {type: "round", legsNumber: 1};

var swHouse = new SoftwareHouse();

swHouse.hire(johnSmith);
swHouse.hire(lassie);
```

```
swHouse.hire(table);

console.log(swHouse.employees.length);      //result:   3
```

Even if we use the `typeof` operator, we will not be able to distinguish persons from other types of objects:

```
console.log(typeof johnSmith);     //result:     object
console.log(typeof lassie);        //result:     object
console.log(typeof lassie);        //result:     object
```

Moreover, the `typeof` operator returns the "object" value also for *null*:

```
console.log(typeof null);     //result:     object
```

So, it is, therefore, completely useless for our purposes.

From data type to instance type

To overcome the limitation of the `typeof` operator on object values, we can impose a constraint on the objects that can be passed to the `hire()` method by accepting only instances of the `Person()` constructor function. So, instead of checking data type, we will check instance type by using the `instanceof` operator:

```
function Person(name, surname) {
  this.name = name;
  this.surname;
}

var johnSmith = new Person("John", "Smith");

console.log(johnSmith instanceof Person);     //result:   true
```

Our definition of the software house will become as follows:

```
class SoftwareHouse {
  constructor() {
    this.employees = [];
  }

  hire(dev) {
    if (dev instanceof Person) {
      this.employees.push(dev);
    } else {
      throw new Error("This software house hires only persons!");
    }
```

```
      }
  }
```

Now, the `hire()` method will accept only persons, throwing an exception if a different type of instance is passed as an argument:

```
var johnSmith = new Person("John", "Smith");
var lassie = {name: "Lassie", breed: "Collie"};
var table = {type: "round", legsNumber: 1};

var swHouse = new SoftwareHouse();

swHouse.hire(johnSmith);
swHouse.hire(lassie);      //result:  Error
swHouse.hire(table);       //result:  Error
```

Beyond the instance type

The solution based on the use of `instanceof` operator might seem quite satisfactory at first sight. However, usually a software house is interested in hiring people who are able to write code, not just any person. From our example's perspective, the software house class might need some method of its employees in order to work properly. In the following code, we added the `createSoftware()` method that uses the `writeCode()` method of its employees to create a new software product:

```
class SoftwareHouse {
  constructor() {
    this.employees = [];
  }

  hire(dev) {
    if (dev instanceof Person) {
      this.employees.push(dev);
    } else {
      throw new Error("This software house hires only persons!");
    }
  }

  createSoftware() {
    var newSoftware = [];
    var employee;
    var module;
    for(var i = 0; i < this.employees.length; i++) {
      employee = this.employees[i];
      module =  employee.writeCode();
```

```
         newSoftware.push(module);      }      return newSoftware;
  }
}
```

Our `Person()` constructor does not define such a method. So if a person object is passed to the `hire()` method, it will be included in the `employees` array, but it will generate an exception when the `createSoftware()` method runs, since the person object does not have a `writeCode()` method.

How can we impose this new constraint on the `hire()` method? We might think of creating a more specialized constructor or class than the `Person()` constructor, for example `Developer`, having the required method. So, the `hire()` method might accept only instances of the `Developer()` constructor. But this might not be sufficient.

In fact we might fail to check whether people can be hired because of multiple inheritance. Let's consider the following definitions:

```
function Developer(name, surname, knownLanguage) {
  Person.apply(this, arguments);
  this.knownLanguage = knownLanguage;
}


Developer.prototype = Object.create(Person.prototype);
Developer.prototype.constructor = Developer;


function Student(name, surname, subjectOfStudy) {
  Person.apply(this, arguments);
  this.subjectOfStudy = subjectOfStudy;
}

Student.prototype = Object.create(Person.prototype);
Student.prototype.constructor = Student;

function DevStudent(name, surname, knownLanguage, subjectOfStudy)  {
  Developer.call(this, name, surname, knownLanguage);
  Student.call(this, name, surname, subjectOfStudy);
}

DevStudent.prototype.writeCode = function() {
  console.log("writing code...");
  return {module: "..."};
};
```

Here, we defined a `Developer()` constructor inheriting from `Person()`, a `Student()` constructor inheriting from `Person()`, and a `DevStudent()` constructor inheriting from `Developer()` and `Student()`. Only instances of `Developer()` will have the `writeCode()` method. But, since the `DevStudent()` constructor inherits from `Developer()`, its instances will have the `writeCode()` method as well.

So, we will expect that instances of both `Developer()` and `DevStudent()` constructors will be valid candidates to be hired by our software house. However, since the `hire()` method is based on the `instanceof` operator, it will fail to hire a `DevStudent()` instance.

In fact a `DevStudent()` instance is not an instance of `Developer()`:

```
var johnSmith = new DevStudent("John", "Smith", "C#",  "JavaScript");

console.log(johnSmith instanceof Student);     //result: false
console.log(johnSmith instanceof Developer);    //result: false
console.log(johnSmith instanceof Person);      //result: false
```

We might set the prototype of the `DevStudent()` constructor to an instance of `Developer()`, but this leads us to make a choice—an instance of `DevStudent()` will be also considered an instance of `Developer()` but not an instance of `Student()`. This might work in this specific case, but might break another case.

Contracts and interfaces

A way to manage interactions between objects is to establish some specific rules so that an object declares what it needs and another object declares what it implements, that is a **contract**. As in a business context, a contract is an agreement between two or more parties for the doing of something specified. For example, in the interaction between two software components, such as objects, we can establish how an object can ask another object to perform some actions in order to achieve a specific goal. With reference to our example of a software house that wants to hire developers, the contract between it and the candidates establishes that the developer must be able to write code.

So, while a contract is a general agreement between two software components in order to achieve a specific goal, an **interface** is the formal terms of the contract, the details of the agreement that the components must be compliant with. We can say that an interface is the concrete part of a contract, a description of the members that an object must have in order to interact with another object for a specific purpose so that their existence can be checked.

Of course all objects have an interface, that is, all of the public methods and properties belonging to that object. But here, we are focusing on the set of members of an object that allow it to be compliant with a contract. So, this set can be all the object's members or just a subset.

Many OOP languages support interfaces by means of specific syntactical constructs. For example, C# and Java have a similar syntax to define an interface. The following code defines an interface that establishes what is needed for an object in order to be hired by our software house:

```
public interface IProgrammer
{
   ModularCode writeCode();
}
```

In this case, the interface requires that an object has a method named `writeCode()` returning an instance of the `ModularCode` class. The interface definition is syntactically similar to a class definition, but it has just public members and no implementation. Mostly, in C#, a naming convention requires that the name of an interface starts with a capitalized i, although it is not a syntactic requirement.

Most strongly typed languages, such as C# and Java, consider an interface like a type definition so that we can use the interface itself wherever we can use a type. For example, we can define a method for hiring developers in the following way:

```
public void Hire(IProgrammer dev)
{
   ...
}
```

In this case, the type system will check whether an object passed to the `Hire()` method implements the required method or, as usually it is said, whether it implements the `IProgrammer` interface.

When we want to define a class that complies with the contract formalized by an interface, we have to declare it using a specific syntactical construct. For example, in C# we can define a class implementing the `IProgrammer` interface as follows:

```
public class DevStudent: IProgrammer {
   ...
}
```

In Java, we will use the following syntax:

```
public class DevStudent implements IProgrammer {
  ...
}
```

It is important to point out that an interface establishes the minimum set of features required to comply with a contract, that is, to interact with another object. An object can implement other methods or properties that are not included in an interface. It also can implement more than one interface.

Duck typing

We introduced the concepts of contract and interface and mentioned how interfaces are defined in two well-known strongly typed languages. Contracts enforced by the implementation of interfaces would allow us to solve the problem of hiring just developers, that is, persons able to write code. However, we saw that interfaces in languages such as C# and Java rely on their type checking system. How can we benefit from contracts and interfaces in JavaScript?

JavaScript neither has a native support of interfaces nor allows us to define new types. Moreover, it is an extremely dynamic language that not only allows to create objects with specific members but also to change their structure at runtime so that we cannot make any assumptions based on instance type or other similar static information. However, we can try to define contracts using the so called **duck typing**.

Duck typing is a programming technique where a contract is established between a function and its caller, requiring the parameters passed in by the caller to have specific members. David Thomas gave this curious name to this technique referring to the colloquial saying *"If it walks like a duck and quacks like a duck, it is a duck."*

Duck typing is not so much a type system as it is an approach to treating objects as if they are certain types based on their behavior rather than their declared type. In other words, rather than checking if an object **is** a duck, we check if it **behaves like** a duck.

Let's see how we can implement duck typing in JavaScript.

A basic approach

The most simple approach to implement duck typing is to check the presence of the required members directly in the method which needs the contract compliance. Referring to our software house example, we can check if the object passed as an argument to the hire() method has a method named writeCode:

```
class SoftwareHouse {
  constructor() {
    this.employees = [];
  }

  hire(dev) {
    if (dev && dev["writeCode"] && dev["writeCode"] instanceof
    Function) {
      this.employees.push(dev);
    } else {
      throw new Error("The argument do not implements writeCode
method")
    }
  }
}
```

We added the highlighted code checking whether a writeCode member exists and if it is a function. If it is not true, an exception is raised. This approach works but it tends to make the hire() method very verbose, especially if more than one member has to be checked.

In a more readable and generic approach, we can define a private function that checks if an object implements a specific method:

```
var  SoftwareHouse = (function() {
  function implement(obj, method) {
    return (obj && obj[method] && obj[method] instanceof
    Function);   }

  return class {
    constructor() {
      this.employees = [];
    }

    hire(dev) {
      if (implement(dev, "writeCode")) {
        this.employees.push(dev);
      } else {
        throw new Error("The argument does not implement writeCode
method")
      }
```

```
        }
    };
})();
```

Here, we included the class definition in an **Immediately Invoked Function Expression**
(**IIFE**) in order to keep private the `implements()` function.

An interface also consists of public properties. For example, in addition to be able to write
code, we can require that our candidates should have a name. This requirement can be
easily checked as shown by the following code:

```
var  SoftwareHouse = (function() {

    function implementsMethod(obj, method) {
        return !!(obj && obj[method] && obj[method] instanceof
        Function);   }
    function implementsProperty(obj, property) {
        return !!(obj && obj[property] && !(obj[property] instanceof
        Function))
    }

    return class {
        constructor() {
            this.employees = [];
        }

        hire(dev) {
            if (implementsMethod(dev, "writeCode") &&
            implementsProperty(dev, "name")) {
                this.employees.push(dev);
            } else {
                throw new Error("The argument is not compatible with the
    required interface")
            }
        }
    };
})();
```

Here, we highlighted the changes to the code, where we implemented two functions to
check if an object implements the required methods and properties: `implementsMethod()`
and `implementsProperty()`.

Note that we used the double not operator in order to force the conversion to Boolean,
when the property or method is undefined.

A general solution

The previous solution requires us to implement private methods to check if an object implements the methods and properties required by a contract. This forces us to replicate quite general code for each class or constructor definition. A more general approach would be desirable.

We can attach the `implementsMethod()` and `implementsProperty()` methods to the prototype of the `Object()` constructor, as shown here:

```
Object.prototype.implementsMethod = function(method) {
  return !!(this[method] && this[method] instanceof Function)
};

Object.prototype.implementsProperty = function(property) {
  return !!(this[property] && !(this[property] instanceof    Function))
};
```

This approach allows us to get these methods for each object so that we can check if an object implements a method or a property very easily:

```
var johnSmith = {name: "John", surname: "Smith", writeCode: function()
{...}};

johnSmith.implementsMethod("name");        //result: true
johnSmith.implementsMethod("writeCode");   //result: true
johnSmith.implementsMethod("writePoems");  //result: false
```

Using this approach, we can rewrite our software house class as follows:

```
class SoftwareHouse {
  constructor() {
    this.employees = [];
  }

  hire(dev) {
    if (dev.implementsMethod("writeCode") &&
dev.implementsProperty("name")) {
      this.employees.push(dev);
    } else {
      throw new Error("The argument is not compatible with the
required interface")
    }
  }
}
```

Even if this is a powerful approach, it should be pointed out that in general attaching methods to the prototype of a built-in constructor is not a good practice. It might clash with other extensions or future additions of the ECMAScript standard.

Emulating Interfaces with duck typing

So far, we found a way as general as possible to check if an object complies with a contract. Such solutions are not true interfaces as per classical OOP languages. In languages such as Java and C#, an interface is a syntactical entity that describes the members an object must implement to comply with a contract. Then, a class declares that it is implementing a specific interface and the type system checks if the declaration of the class actually does what it is saying. In JavaScript, we cannot rely on a mechanism like this, we have no syntactical entity to declare interfaces nor a type system to check compliance. However, we can emulate interfaces in some way letting the code look more similar to classical OOP interfaces.

In order to obtain an interface-like approach, we define a class that emulates an interface declaration and check if an object implements it. Let's take a look at the code:

```
class Interface {
  constructor(name, methods=[], properties=[]) {
    this.name = name;
    this.methods = [];
    this.properties = [];

    for (let i = 0, len = methods.length; i < len; i++) {
      if (typeof methods[i] !== 'string') {
        throw new Error("Interface constructor expects method
        names to be passed in as a string.");
      }
      this.methods.push(methods[i]);
    }

    for (let i = 0, len = properties.length; i < len; i++) {
      if (typeof properties[i] !== 'string') {
        throw new Error("Interface constructor expects property
        names to be passed in as a string.");
      }
      this.properties.push(properties[i]);
    }
  }

  isImplementedBy(obj) {
    var methodsLen = this.methods.length;
```

```
        var propertiesLen = this.properties.length;
        var currentMember;

        if (obj) {
          //check methods
          for (let i = 0; i < methodsLen; i++) {
            currentMember = this.methods[i];
            if (!obj[currentMember] || typeof obj[currentMember] !==
            "function") {
              throw new Error("The object does not implement the
              interface " + this.name + ". Method " + currentMember +
              " not found.");
            }
          }

          //check properties
          for (let i = 0; i < propertiesLen; i++) {
            currentMember = this.properties[i];
            if (!obj[currentMember] || typeof obj[currentMember] ===
            "function") {
              throw new Error("The object does not implement the
              interface " + this.name + ". Property " + currentMember
              + " not found.");
            }
          }
        } else {
          throw new Error("No object to check!");
        }
      }
    }
```

In essential parts, the class constructor takes three arguments: the name of the interface, an array of method names, and an array of property names. By creating an instance of the Interface class, we are declaring the existence of a contract requiring the implementation of the methods and properties passed as arguments. During the instance construction, the method and the property names are stored in the property's methods and properties of the instance itself.

The isImplementedBy() method takes an object as argument and checks if it complies with the contract described by the interface, that is, checks if it implements all required methods and properties. If at least one of the required members is not among the members implemented by the object, an exception is thrown saying which member is missing.

Of course, we can implement the `Interface` class as a constructor function for backward compatibility. The following code shows the equivalent version without ECMAScript 6 syntax:

```
function Interface(name, methods, properties) {
  "use strict";

  methods = methods || [];
  properties = properties || [];

  this.name = name;
  this.methods = [];
  this.properties = [];

  for (let i = 0, len = methods.length; i < len; i++) {
    if (typeof methods[i] !== 'string') {
      throw new Error("Interface constructor expects method names
      to be passed in as a string.");
    }
    this.methods.push(methods[i]);
  }

  for (let i = 0, len = properties.length; i < len; i++) {
    if (typeof properties[i] !== 'string') {
      throw new Error("Interface constructor expects property
      names to be passed in as a string.");
    }
    this.properties.push(properties[i]);
  }
}


Interface.prototype.isImplementedBy = function(obj) {
  "use strict";
  var methodsLen = this.methods.length;
  var propertiesLen = this.properties.length;
  var currentMember;

  if (obj) {
    //check methods
    for (let i = 0; i < methodsLen; i++) {
      currentMember = this.methods[i];
      if (!obj[currentMember] || typeof obj[currentMember] !==
      "function") {
        throw new Error("The object does not implement the
        interface " + this.name + ". Method " +currentMember + "
        not found.");
      }
```

```
      }

    //check properties
    for (let i = 0; i < propertiesLen; i++) {
      currentMember = this.properties[i];
      if (!obj[currentMember] || typeof obj[currentMember] ===
      "function") {
        throw new Error("The object does not implement the
        interface " + this.name + ". Property " + currentMember +
        " not found.");
      }
    }
  } else {
    throw new Error("No object to check!");
  }
};
```

Now, we can easily create an interface requiring the constraints an object must comply with in order to interact with other objects. For example, we can create an interface that establishes the criteria by which a candidate can be hired:

```
var IHireable = new Interface("IHireable", ["writeCode"],  ["name"]);
```

Here, we created the interface `IHireable` requiring that an object must implement a method named `writeCode` and a property named `name`. Note how we have taken the naming convention borrowed from C#, although it is not mandatory.

Now, our software house class definition is more compact and readable and its method `hire()` will get any object with a name and will be able to write the code:

```
class SoftwareHouse {
  constructor() {
    this.employees = [];
  }

  hire(dev) {
    IHireable.isImplementedBy(dev);
    this.employees.push(dev);
  }
}
```

As a result, only if an object implements the `IHireable` interface, it will be pushed in to the `employees` array.

Multiple interface implementation

As we said so far, an object implementing an interface can also have other methods and properties that are not required by the specific interface. It can also implement multiple interfaces without breaking the contract. Let's make an example of multiple interface implementation by considering that our software house needs a developer to be also a team leader. Team leadership is a cross competence, so it not necessarily tied to the developer role. Instead of including the team leadership feature in the IHireable interface, we can define a new specific interface:

```
var ITeamLeadership = new Interface("ITeamLeadership",  ["delegateTo",
"motivate"], ["team"]);
```

We defined the ITeamLeadership interface, which requires the implementation of two methods, delegateTo() and motivate(), and one property, team.

Now, our SoftwareHouse class should check the implementation of both interfaces before hiring a new developer:

```
class SoftwareHouse {
  constructor() {
    this.employees = [];
  }

  hire(dev) {
    IHireable.isImplementedBy(dev);
    ITeamLeadership.isImplementedBy(dev);
    this.employees.push(dev);
  }
}
```

As we can see, checking if a developer implements both interfaces is simply made by executing the isImplementedBy() method of both interfaces.

The following is an example of checking the implementation of the IHireable and ITeamLeaderhip interfaces:

```
var johnSmith = {
  name: "John",
  surname: "Smith",
  writeCode: function() {...},
  delegateTo: function() {...},
  motivate: function() {...},
  team: []};

var swHouse = new SoftwareHouse();
```

```
swHouse.hire(johnSmith);

console.log(swHouse.employees.indexOf(johnSmith)); //result:    0
```

Duck typing and polymorphism

Often duck typing is assimilated to polymorphism, since it allows in some way to uniformly manage different type of objects. However, they are different concepts.

Polymorphism is a concept found on types whereas duck typing is found on contracts. With polymorphism, it is important **what an object is** and not how it behaves. In duck typing, it is important **how an object behaves**. Duck typing is more tied to the concept of objects that interact, rather than objects that are of a certain type.

However, duck typing can help to implement solutions that strongly typed languages resolve with true polymorphism. Let's consider an example where our software house wants to implement a method that creates a list of full names of all the employees. The list of employees of the software house can contain not only developers but also salesmen, business analysts, system architects, and so on. Each of these categories of objects may have different ways to store their full name. For example, the following could be the class definitions of a developer, salesman, and business analyst:

```
class Developer {
  constructor(name, surname) {
    this.name = name;
    this.surname = surname;
  }
}

class Salesman {
  constructor(name, surname) {
    this.firstName = name;
    this.secondName = surname;
  }
}

class BusinessAnalyst {
  constructor(fullName) {
    this.fullName = fullNname;
  }
}
```

These different ways to define the name and surname of the employees of our software house force the `SoftwareHouse` class to implement the listing method as in the following:

```
class SoftwareHouse {
  constructor() {
    this.employees = [];
  }

  listEmployees() {
    var employeesLen = this.employees.length;
    var currentEmployee;

    for(var i = 0; i < employeesLen; i++) {
      currentEmployee =  this.employees[i];

      if (currentEmployee instanceof Developer) {
        console.log(currentEmployee.name + " " +
currentEmployee.surname);
      } else if (currentEmployee instanceof Salesman) {
        console.log(currentEmployee.firstName + " " +
currentEmployee.secondName);
      } else if (currentEmployee instanceof BusinessAnalyst) {
        console.log(currentEmployee.fullName);
      }
    }
  }
}
```

The `listEmployees()` method checks the type of instance of each employee and writes to the console their full name based on the specific structure of the object. This code is very ugly and difficult to maintain. If the software house decides to hire a new type of employee, such as system architects, we should change the method's implementation in order to check this new type of employee and compose its full name.

A better way to manage such a situation is to use duck typing by enforcing each class to implement a `getFullName()` method. In this way, each type of employee will have the responsibility to give its full name. Let's take a look at how we can implement all that.

First of all, let's create an interface to define our contract:

```
var IFullName = new Interface("IFullName", ["getFullName"]);
```

Thanks to this new approach, the code of our `SoftwareHouse` class will be more simple and maintainable:

```
class SoftwareHouse {
  constructor() {
```

```
      this.employees = [];
    }

  listEmployees() {
    var employeesLen = this.employees.length;
    var currentEmployee;

    for(var i = 0; i < employeesLen; i++) {
      currentEmployee =  this.employees[i];

      IFullName.isImplementedBy(currentEmployee);
      console.log(currentEmployee.getFullName());
    }
  }
}
```

This approach will correctly manage possible new types of employees that implement the `IFullName` interface. Obviously, checking of the interface implementation should be done when a new employee is added to the `employees` array, for example, in the `hire()` method we have implemented in previous examples.

This example shows how we can use duck typing to overcome the limitation of true polymorphism support in JavaScript.

Summary

This chapter focused on using duck typing instead of relying on type checking. We see how the dynamic nature of JavaScript and its type system do not allow us to process objects in a reliable way. The structure of an object can change dynamically and establishing the type of instance of an object that may be very difficult, for example, when multiple inheritance is applied. Therefore, we introduced the concept of a contract between objects and the support of interfaces provided by classical OOP languages.

Since JavaScript does not support interfaces, we explored the duck typing technique in order to describe and check the contract's compliance. Duck typing allows us to process objects focusing on how an object behaves instead of relying on what it is and what its type is.

Then, we elaborated an approach that allows us to emulate classical OOP interfaces and make some considerations about the relationship between duck typing and polymorphism.

In the next chapter, we will discuss different ways to create objects by exploring some of the most well-known design patterns.

6
Advanced Object Creation

The JavaScript Object-Oriented Programming model has no classes, and it is directly based on objects, whose creation process may happen in different ways. We already talked about the standard ways in which we can create objects, but in some situations, we may need a more sophisticated approach.

This chapter introduces the group of design patterns known as **creational patterns**, that is, patterns concerning the creation of an object in a structural way. After a reminder on the standard ways to create objects, we will show you how to take advantage of the following patterns:

- Singleton pattern
- Factory pattern
- Abstract factory pattern
- Builder pattern
- Object pool pattern

Creating objects

We have seen in previous chapters the different ways JavaScript allows us to create objects. We can use the literal notation to create objects in an extremely easy manner or we can apply a constructor function, we can create instances of a `class` definition or invoke the `Object.create()` method. Each approach has its benefits and drawbacks, and we can use what we consider most suitable for our needs.

The literal notation is the easiest approach. We can just create an object by defining its properties and methods between curly braces:

```
var johnSmith = { name: "John", surname: "Smith"};
```

The positive side of this approach is its simplicity. The negative side is that we need to specify each property and method and it is not suitable to create many similar objects. Usually, its use is limited to the creation of a single object.

The creation of objects based on constructor functions or classes allows us to define an object template from which we can create as many objects as we want:

```
function Person(name, surname) {
  this.name = name;
  this.surname = surname;
}

class Person {
  constructor(name, surname) {
    this.name = name;
    this.surname = surname;
  }
}
```

Regardless of the approach used to define our template, we can create objects using the `new` operator:

```
var johnSmith = new Person("John", "Smith");
```

As we already discussed in Chapter 4, *Inheriting and Creating Mixins*, using constructor functions and classes allows us to optimize memory usage by sharing the method's code among their instances, thanks to prototype and inheritance. However, many have criticized the `new` operator because it appears as misleading since it is the same operator usually used to create an object from a class in classical OOP languages. They say that the `new` operator is neither coherent with a classless approach of JavaScript OOP nor with the functional nature of the language.

The alternative approach is based on the `Object.create()` method. Like constructor functions and classes, it allows us to create objects from a prototype and is easier to understand and more coherent with JavaScript's nature:

```
var johnSmith = Object.create();
johnSmith.name = "John";
johnSmith.surname = "Smith";
```

However, not always, these standard approaches to create objects are suitable in certain contexts. Sometimes the object creation process may be complex or require a high level of flexibility. In these situations, we can use some of the most known design patterns to achieve a solution to our specific needs.

Design patterns and object creation

One of the most popular topics in Object-Oriented Programming is **design patterns**. They are known as reusable solutions to commonly occurring software design problems. Each pattern is identified by a name and describes a situation where components need to interact with each other to achieve a specific goal.

 Design patterns became popular in the mid-nineties after the publishing of the book *Design Patterns: Elements of Reusable Object-Oriented Software* by the so-called Gang of Four (GoF): Erich Gamma, Richard Helm, Ralph Johnson, and John Vlissides.

The patterns are described so that they can be reused regardless of the language used to implement it. However, the original patterns and the subsequent ones added in the following years were mainly described for classical Object-Oriented languages. So often, they are described in terms of classes, interfaces, and other traditional constructs. Due to lack of native support for some classical OOP constructs, in JavaScript often we have to adapt them to the dynamic nature of the language, obtaining in many cases a simplification.

Patterns are usually categorized in groups of similar goals. For example, the original design patterns proposed by the GoF had three categories: creational, structural, and behavioral. In this chapter, you will learn how to implement in JavaScript some of the most known patterns concerning the object creation activity, while we will explore some other design patterns throughout the book.

Creating a singleton

Sometimes, we may need to have a single occurrence of an object throughout the application life. Consider, for example, a configuration manager or a cache manager. Since they provide a global point of access to an internal or external resource, they need to be implemented in a way so that only one instance must exist, that is, they need to be implemented as a **singleton**.

The singleton pattern is one of the simplest design patterns—it involves only one entity which is responsible for making sure it creates not more than one instance and provides a global point of access to itself. For a class-based language, this means that a class can be instantiated only one time and any attempt to create a new instance of the class returns the instance already created.

In JavaScript, we can create objects through the literal notation, so any such object is already a singleton:

```
var johnSingleton = {
    name: "John",
    surname: "Singleton"
};
```

So, why do we need to implement this design pattern?

In the preceding example, we created an object which, if created in the global context of an application, is accessible from everywhere in the application. However, we are not sure that this object will actually be used during the application life. If a particular execution flow of the application does not use our object, we unnecessarily wasted the system's resources. Moreover, if we need some data or any preprocessing must be performed before the creation of the object's instance, we need to delay the object creation. Finally, if our object has to manage a private state, using a literal object is not the best way.

The mysterious behavior of constructors

So, how can we implement singletons in JavaScript? Before we go into that, let's explore an interesting behavior of constructor functions.

Usually, when we define a constructor, we do not specify a return value. The new operator causes the return of a new object instance from the current value of this. If we create a constructor returning a primitive value, such as a string or a number, it will be ignored:

```
function Person(name, surname) {
  this.name = name;
  this.surname = surname;

  return "This is a person";
}

var johnSmith = new Person("John", "Smith");

console.log(johnSmith.name);        //John
console.log(johnSmith.surname);     //Smith
```

In this example, the constructor returns a string, but we have no effect on the creation of a new object nor get any trace of the string returned by the constructor.

If our constructor returns an object, it will be returned and the object bound to the `this` keyword will be lost:

```
function Person(name, surname) {
  this.name = name;
  this.surname = surname;

  return { firstName: name, secondName: surname };
}

var johnSmith = new Person("John", "Smith");

console.log(johnSmith.name);        //undefined
console.log(johnSmith.surname);     //undefined
console.log(johnSmith.firstName);   //John
console.log(johnSmith.secondName);  //Smith
```

Here, our new object will have the properties defined in the returned object, not the properties attached to `this`.

Singletons

With this constructor's behavior in mind, let's take a look at how we can implement a singleton in JavaScript. Suppose, for example, we need an identifier generator returning unique values, we can define it as follows:

```
var IdGenerator = (function() {
  var instance;
  var counter = 0;

  var Constructor = function() {
    if (!instance) {
      instance = this;
    }

    return instance;
  };

  Constructor.prototype.newId = function() {
  return ++counter;
};

  return Constructor;
})();
```

We used an IIFE in order to keep private the unique instance of the object created by the constructor and the `counter` variable that tracks the current value of the generated identifier. The interesting part of this code is the constructor definition. We check if an instance has been defined, if this is not the case, we associate the current value of `this` to the `instance` variable, otherwise, we return the current value of the `instance` variable. This ensures that an object instance will be created just when it's needed, and the same object will be returned each time an attempt to create a new generator will be made:

```
var g = new IdGenerator();

console.log(g.newId());         //result:    1
console.log(g.newId());         //result:    2

var g1 = new IdGenerator();

console.log(g1.newId());        //result:    3
```

In the constructor definition, we attached the `newId()` method to the constructor's prototype, as usual. However in this case, it is not strictly necessary since we will have just one object instance all over the application, so we could attach the method to `this`.

Of course, we can define our singleton using the ES6 `class` syntax as shown here:

```
var IdGenerator = (function(){
    var instance;
    var counter = 0;

    return class {
      constructor() {
        if (!instance) {
          instance = this;
        }

        return instance;
      }

      newId() {
        return ++counter;
      }
    };
})();
```

When to use singletons?

When we introduced singletons, we provided some examples in which they can be used. Not only did we mention the configuration and cache managers, but also mentioned that the log manager could be a good candidate. However, the choice to implement the singleton pattern must be made carefully, otherwise, we risk creating objects that pollute the global environment and can become a bottleneck in the system. From a certain point of view, we can consider singletons like global variables whose drawbacks we all know. In particular, its globally availability may create tight coupling among the various components of the application, reducing their reusability.

So, in order to decide whether to implement an object as a singleton, we can ask ourselves if it is really necessary and possibly use it with caution.

An object factory

In some contexts, we need to create different types of objects, but we wish to manage their creation in a uniform way. Consider, for example, a word processor that need to allow the user to add elements to a document: words, paragraphs, images, sections, and so on. Each type of object will match a class or constructor that will create the required object and will put it on the document. This means that the document manager needs to know how to create each type of object. Moreover, when a new type of element is added to the word processor's capability, say tables, the document manager must be modified in order to learn how to create these new elements.

In these cases, the **factory pattern** can help us set up a more effective approach.

Understanding factories

In general, a factory is an entity (a function and an object) used to create objects, as in the following basic example:

```
function createPerson(name, surname) {
  return {name: name, surname: surname};
}
```

Unlike a constructor function, this factory returns the object it creates without using the `new` operator:

```
var johnSmith = createPerson("John", "Smith");
```

This is a very minimal example of a factory and might not clearly explain its usefulness, apart from the purely functional approach. The purpose of a factory is to abstract the details of object creation from object use and it is particularly useful when the object creation process is relatively complex.

In the classical definition of the factory pattern, we have three actors involved:

- **The client**: This is the object that needs another object of a specific category
- **The factory**: This is the object able to generate objects of a number of categories
- **The product**: This is the object created by the factory and returned to the client

We can represent graphically the interactions between the actors of the factory patterns as in the following diagram:

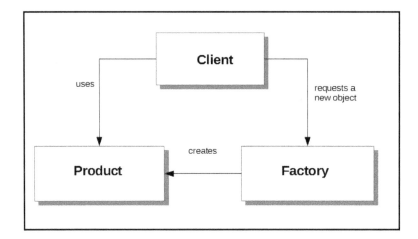

In order to make more understandable this abstract definition, let's go into an example to better explain.

Consider a slightly different definitions of the `Developer` and `SoftwareHouse` classes introduced in the previous chapters:

```
class Developer {
  constructor(skills, benefits) {
    this.skills = ["programming"].concat(skills);
    this.salary = 40000;
    this.benefits = ["computer"].concat(benefits);
  }
}
```

```
class SoftwareHouse {
  constructor() {
    this.employees = [];
  }

  hireDeveloper() {
    var dev = new Developer(["JavaScript"], ["smartphone"]);
    this.employees.push(dev);
  }
}
```

The `Developer` class defines objects with some default features tied to its intrinsic role and other features specific for each instance and passed to the constructor. The `SoftwareHouse` class has a `hireDeveloper()` method that creates a new developer and adds it to the list of employees.

Suppose that the company grew so that it needs to hire people with different roles: salesmen, business analysts, system engineers, and so on, we cannot use the same `hireDeveloper()` method for all types of role, because it should be changed to manage different type of objects. To solve this issue, we can implement different methods, one for each type of role we need to hire, as follows:

```
class Salesman {
  constructor(skills, benefits) {
    this.skills = ["selling"].concat(skills);
    this.salary = 50000;
    this.benefits = ["computer"].concat(benefits);
  }
}

class BusinessAnalyst {
  constructor(skills, benefits) {
    this.skills = ["analyzing"].concat(skills);
    this.salary = 60000;
    this.benefits = ["computer"].concat(benefits);
  }
}

class SoftwareHouse {
  constructor() {
    this.employees = [];
  }

  hireDeveloper() {
    var dev = new Developer(["JavaScript"], ["smartphone"]);
    this.employees.push(dev);
  }
```

```
hireSalesman() {
    var sm = new Salesman(["communication"], ["smartphone",      "car"]);
    this.employees.push(sm);
}

hireBusinessAnalyst() {
    var ba = new BusinessAnalyst(["communication", "writing"],
    ["smartphone", "tablet"]);
    this.employees.push(ba);
}
}
```

Each method creates a specific object and adds it to the employees array.

This approach pollutes the class with methods that really have nothing to do with its core
goal-creating software. Moreover, if we want to hire a new role, we need to add a new
method to the SoftwareHouse class, getting worse even more the situation. A better
approach is to delegate to a specialized object the task to hire people on behalf of the
SoftwareHouse-a RecruitmentAgency, the factory:

```
class RecruitmentAgency {

    getStaffMember(role, skills, benefits) {
        var member;

        switch(role .toLowerCase()) {
            case "dev":
                member = new Developer(skills, benefits);
                break;
            case "sale":
                member = new Salesman(skills, benefits);
                break;
            case "ba":
                member = new BusinessAnalyst(skills, benefits);
                break;
            default:
                throw new Error("Unable to hire people for the role " +
                role)
        }

        return member;
    }
}
```

The `RecruitmentAgency` class is a factory whose method `getStaffMember()` uses a string passed as the first parameter to detect which type of role it must hire. For each role, the correspondent constructor function is invoked, such as `Developer()`, `Salesman()`, and so on. With the proper skills, it benefits parameters. With this approach, we give a factory the responsibility of creating the objects instead of creating them inside the client.

The `SoftwareHouse` class will use the `RecruitmentAgency` factory simply calling the `getStaffMember()` method by passing the desired role and specific parameters, as in the following example:

```
var agency = new RecruitmentAgency();

var newDevStaffMember = agency.getStaffMember("dev", ["C++",  "C#"],
["tablet"]);
```

The application of the factory pattern frees our class from the responsibility of getting objects whose creation process may be complex and out of its main goal.

Factory with constructor registration

The implementation of the factory we have just shown is the most simple and intuitive. However, it has a main drawback: when we need to add a new role we should modify the `RecruitmentAgency` class. It may be acceptable in situations where these changes happen very seldomly, but we can do better by decoupling the factory from the concrete object creator functions.

Let's rewrite the `RecruitmentAgency` class as follows:

```
class RecruitmentAgency {
  constructor() {
    this.objConstructors = {};
  }

  register(role, constructor) {
    this.objConstructors[role] = constructor;
  }

  getStaffMember(role, skills, benefits) {
    var objConstructor =  this.objConstructors[role];
    var member;

    if (objConstructor) member = new objConstructor(skills,
    benefits);
```

```
        return member;
    }
}
```

As we can see, the `RecruitmentAgency` class defines an `objConstructors` property in its constructor. This property will contain the references to all constructor functions or classes stored as properties of an object. The `register()` method allows us to register a constructor by assigning it to a property of the `objConstructors` property. Finally, the `getStaffMember()` method got rid of the `switch` statement and now uses the `objConstructors` object to find the correct constructor for the requested role.

So, we have a registration phase that attaches the constructors to the factory, as in the following example:

```
var agency = new RecruitmentAgency();

agency.register("dev", Developer);
agency.register("ba", BusinessAnalyst);
agency.register("sale", Salesman);
```

With this approach, the addition of a new constructor will simply require the function definition and its registration to the factory with a new role code.

The abstract factory

An evolution of the factory pattern is the **abstract factory pattern**. This pattern builds on the factory pattern since it returns a factory instead of an object. In fact, sometimes it is called a or a *factory of factories*. In this pattern, we find the following actors:

- **The client**: As in the factory pattern, this is the object that needs another object of a specific category
- **The abstract factory**: This is the object that returns a concrete factory
- **The concrete factory**: It is the factory returned by the abstract factory able to create objects of a number of categories
- **The product**: This is the object created by the concrete factory and used by the client

The following diagram represents the interactions between the actors involved in the pattern:

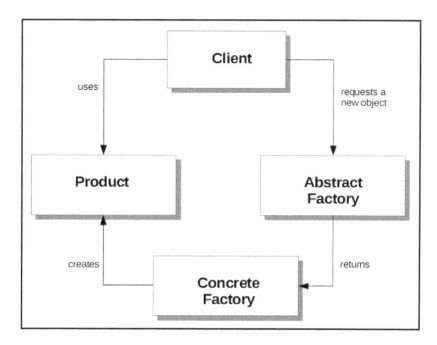

In order to explain how this pattern works, let's modify our example of the recruiting agency considering a case where we have more agencies, each one specialized in recruiting staff members in a specific area, such as development, sales, and so on. Inside each area, they can detect and hire people with specific skills, for example JavaScript, C#, or SQL skills for the development area.

We can imagine that our `SoftwareHouse` class wants to contact a specialized recruitment agency for its hiring needs, and it can obtain this agency through an abstract factory.

Let's model this case with the following class:

```
class RecruitmentAgencyAbstractFactory {

  constructor() {
    this.agencyFactories = {};
  }

  register(area, agencyFactory) {
    this.agencyFactories[area] = agencyFactory;
  }
```

```
  getAgency (area) {
    return new this.agencyFactories[area];
  }
}
```

The class defines the `agencyFactories` property in its constructor, with the same goal we have seen in the `RecruitmentAgency` implementation. The `register()` method allows an agency factory to be registered on the `agencyFactories` property with a specific area code. The `getAgency()` method returns the factory identified by the area code passed as a parameter.

The registration phase allows the agency factories to be registered in the abstract factory:

```
var agencyFinder = new RecruitmentAgencyAbstractFactory();

agencyFinder.register("dev", DevAgency);
agencyFinder.register("sales", SalesAgency);
agencyFinder.register("ba", BusinessAnalystAgency);
```

Each agency factory will be focused on returning specialized staff members. For example, the agency factory specialized in recruiting developers can be implemented as follows:

```
class DevAgency {
  getStaffMember(skills, benefits) {
    return new Developer(skills, benefits);
  }
}
```

In a similar way, we can implement the other agencies.

With this infrastructure, the `SoftwareHouse` class will use our abstract factory to get an agency specialized in an area, as shown by the following example:

```
var devAgency = agencyFinder.getAgency("dev");
var newDevMember = devAgency.getStaffMember(["JavaScript"],  ["phone"]);
```

In this example, we seek out an agency specialized in hiring developers and then ask for a developer with JavaScript skills providing a phone as an employee benefit.

The builder pattern

Another way to delegate the task of creating objects to another object is using the **builder pattern**. This pattern is used to create complex objects that usually require a step-by-step approach.

In the classical definition, this pattern involves the following actors:

- **The client**: This is the object that needs a new object
- **The director**: This is the actor who knows how to create an object, that is, it knows the necessary steps to get an object built
- **The builder**: This actor actually builds the object by providing methods used by the director
- **The product**: It is the resulting object built by the builder under the control of the director

In a nutshell, the client asks for a product from the director, who creates it by means of the builder. The following diagram shows the interaction between the actors:

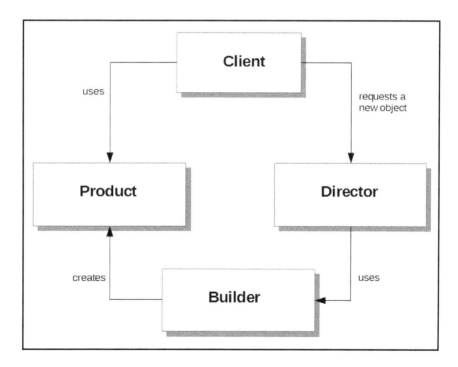

Let's map this pattern in our software house context.

Suppose that our `SoftwareHouse` class has a `createSoftware()` method that takes a software specification and returns an application. The software development is a complex task that involves several steps. Usually, it is not a good idea to start to develop it without a plan and a work organization. So, it should be better to set up a developer team (the builder) and assign it to a project manager (the director). Translating this scenario to code we would get something similar to the following:

```
class SoftwareHouse {
  constructor() {...}

  createSoftware(specs) {
    var webSwBuilderTeam = new WebSwBuilderTeam();
    var projectManager = new ProjectManager(webSwBuilderTeam);
    return projectManager.buildSoftware(specs);
  }
}
```

Inside the `createSoftware()` method, we create an instance of a web developer's team (`WebSwBuilderTeam()`) and pass it to the constructor of a project manager (`ProjectManager()`). Then, we call the `buildSoftware()` method of the project manager object passing to it the software specification. As we can see, the `SoftwareHouse` class, which has the role of the client in the pattern's scenario, does not know the details about how to build a software. It simply provides a development team and delegates to the project manager the task of controlling and ensuring that the software is developed following the specifications.

It is worth nothing that in our example we used an instance of `WebSwBuilderTeam()` to represent a development team specialized in building web applications, but the software house can use different development teams based on the type of application to develop: web, mobile, desktop, and so on. Of course, all these teams need to have a common interface in order to be uniformly used by the project manager.

Let's see how the `ProjectManager` class may be implemented:

```
class ProjectManager {
  constructor(builderTeam) {
    IDevelopmentTeam.isImplementedBy(builderTeam);
    this.builderTeam = builderTeam;
  }

  buildSoftware(specs) {
    var detailedSpecs = this.builderTeam.analyze(specs);
    var code = this.builderTeam.writeCode(detailedSpecs);
    var testedCode = this.builderTeam.test(code);
```

```
        return this.builderTeam.deploy(testedCode);
    }
}
```

In the constructor, we want to be sure that the team passed as a parameter complies with the contract defined by the interface `IDevelopmentTeam`, borrowing the approach used in the previous chapter. If the team is valid, it is taken as the current development team.

The `buildSoftware()` method takes the software specification as an input and uses the methods provided by the current development team in order to develop the software.

The `ProjectManager` class is responsible for the development of the software, and it can change the execution flow of the team's methods on the basis of the specification or by following other criteria.

When to use the builder pattern?

We have seen that the builder pattern allows a client to ignore the steps behind the creation of complex objects. It assigns to another object (the director) the responsibility for following each step of the creation process.

Typical scenarios in which we can apply the builder pattern include the conversion of documents in different formats. For each format, we implement a specific builder that exposes methods to convert paragraphs, format information, page layouts, and so on. The director will use these methods to convert a document passed as a parameter by following its structure.

In classical Object-Oriented Programming contexts, such as in Java, the builder pattern is often used to refactor a class with a constructor with many parameters, some mandatory and other optionals, such as the following:

```
Pizza(int size) {...}
Pizza(int size, boolean cheese) {...}
Pizza(int size, boolean cheese, boolean tomato) {...}
Pizza(int size, boolean cheese, boolean tomato, boolean bacon)  {...}
```

These kinds of constructors are difficult to read and error prone due to the presence of many parameters of the same type:

```
Pizza pizza = new Pizza(10, true, false, true);
```

By defining a builder with methods that allows us to set specific parameters make the code more readable, even if more verbose:

```
Pizza pizza = new Pizza.Builder(10).addCheese().addBacon();
```

Although we can apply this approach in JavaScript, it might not be a good idea. In JavaScript, a more simple approach is usually used to manage this situation—an option object. Thanks to the dynamic nature of JavaScript objects, we can create a literal with the only options we want to pass to the constructor, as shown here:

```
var pizza = new Pizza({size: 10, cheese: true, bacon; true});
```

The constructor function will apply just the properties of the options object leaving the other properties to their default value:

```
function Pizza(options) {
  this.size = options.size || 5;
  this.cheese = options.chees || false;
  this.tomato = options.tomato || false;
  this.bacon = options.bacon || false;
}
```

Comparing factory and builder patterns

The factory pattern and the builder pattern have a similar goal and may be confused if they are not properly understood. Both patterns allow to create objects, but each one has its own peculiarity and scope of application.

In particular, the factory pattern focuses on object creation on the basis of a category or other ways to group objects. When a client asks an object to a factory, it specifies the category of object it needs. However, all objects created by the factory implement the same interface or inherit from the same object so that the client can manage them in the same way without actually knowing its real type.

The builder pattern focuses on building complex objects. Unlike the factories, the builders of the builder pattern do not always return the same type of object. They may return (and it happens often) different type of objects. Consider a document converter—it returns different types of objects based on the requested output format.

Moreover, a factory returns an object as a result of one simple call to a constructor function, while in the builder pattern the resulting object is constructed by the director in multiple steps.

These aspects have to be taken into account when deciding which pattern to apply to a design problem.

Recycling objects with an object pool

Sometimes, the creation of objects may be so complex that it can affect the application performance. Consider, for example, when the creation of an object requires a call across the network to a remote API or when the object's setup need expensive computational resources. Also, the frequent creation and destruction of objects may affect the overall performance, since the garbage collector is frequently involved.

In these situations, it would be better to extend the object's life as much as possible. In other words, we may maintain an object alive instead of discarding it when a client no longer needs it. Here, we can use the **object pool pattern**.

The object pool pattern involves the following actors:

- **A client**: This is the object that needs another object
- **An object pool**: This is the component responsible for managing a set of reusable objects
- **A reusable object**: This is the object required by the client

In simple terms, the object pool pattern allows to retain a set of unused objects of the same type. When a client needs a new object, rather than creating a new one by itself, it instead recycles one of the unused objects from the pool. When the client no longer need the object, rather than releasing it to the main memory, it is returned to the pool. Note that the object will not be garbage collected, since it is never deleted from the code. The following picture shows how the actors of this pattern interact with each other:

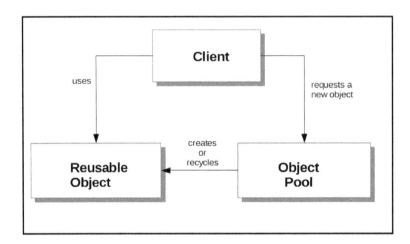

Let's take a look how we can implement an object pool in our software house model. Suppose that objects such as trainers are very expensive to create, it is not convenient to create and destroy this type of objects, however, we can manage their lifecycle inside an object pool.

The following code shows a simple example of object pool implementation:

```
var ObjectPool = (function(){
  var instance;
  var objConstructor;
  var objPool = [];

  return class {
    constructor(objConstr) {
      if (!instance) {
        objConstructor = objConstr;
        instance = this;
      }

      return instance;
    }
```

```
  get() {
    var obj;

    if (objPool.length == 0) {
      obj = new objConstructor();
    } else {
      obj = objPool.pop();
    }

    return obj;
  }

  recycle(obj) {
    objPool.push(obj);
  }
};
})();
```

We can see that the object is a singleton. It is necessary since we need a unique entry point to access shared resources.

In addition to the `instance` variable that allows us to manage the singleton, we have two other private variables: the `objConstructor` variable, which will store the constructor function of the objects be created; and the `objPool`, an array that will actually contain the reusable objects.

The pool's constructor takes an object constructor as an argument. This is the constructor to be used in order to create new instances of objects when the pool is empty.

The object pool has two methods: `get()`, the method that returns an available object from the pool, and `recycle()`, that pushes an unused object in the pool. The `get()` method has also the responsibility for creating a new object when the pool is empty. Let's consider the `Trainer` class whose objects we want to manage with the Object Pool Pattern:

```
class Trainer {
  explain() {...}
  show() {...}
  exercise() {...}
}
```

The class is very simplified since it is not so relevant for our purpose. Now we can create a pool of trainer using the following code:

```
var trainerPool = new ObjectPool(Trainer);
```

The `trainerPool` object will be an object pool specializing in managing `Trainer` instances. The pool will initially be empty, and the first requests to create new objects will return new `Trainer` objects leaving the pool still empty:

```
var trainer1 = trainerPool.get();
var trainer2 = trainerPool.get();
```

The pool will have some entries when a client releases its `Trainer` object using the `recycle()` method:

```
trainerPool.recycle(trainer1);
```

Now, when a client requests a new `Trainer` object, the pool will not create a new one, but will return the one in the pool:

```
var trainer3 = trainerPool.get();

console.log(trainer1 == trainer2);  //false
console.log(trainer1 == trainer3);  //true
```

This avoids a possible expensive creation cost, a frequent involvement of the garbage collector, and a reduction in memory fragmentation. Of course, the reuse of an object in the pool is possible only if it has no state, that is, its private variables and public properties do not change. If it is not the case, the objects to be stored in the pool require an initialization method that allows to it reset its state to the initial value.

In our simple example, we have not placed any constraint on the management of the pool. It is implemented as an array that can grow without limits. In real-life situations, the pool is configured so that it cannot grow over a maximum size, avoiding to run out of memory.

Moreover, in our example we defined an object pool that can contain only one type of objects, `Trainer`. Once created, an object pool by passing a specific object constructor or class, we cannot store objects of another type. In practical implementation, we should allow one object pool to manage different type of objects or allow the creation of multiple object pools managing different type of objects.

During the design of a real-life object pool, we must take into account various policies that allow to manage the memory as best as possible. For instance, we must remember that unused objects remain in memory forever, so we might think of a way to destroy them and to free memory after a certain amount of lifetime.

Summary

In this chapter, we explored different ways of creating objects. We started recalling the basic ways to create objects in JavaScript and then discussed how some design patterns can help us to create more effective code. We have seen how to create singletons and warned about their abuse. Then we analyzed the factory pattern and its variant abstract factory pattern-both allows us to delegate to a specialized object (the factory) the task of creating objects belonging to a specific category. The builder pattern can be useful when creating some kind of objects is a complex process that consists of many steps. In this case, we use a special object (the director) that uses other objects (the builders) to actually create the object. Finally, we talked about the object pool pattern, which allows us to reuse objects avoiding a negative impact on the application performance when the creation of a type of object, is too expensive or when we have frequent creation and destruction of objects.

In the next chapter, we will continue the exploration of the design patterns focusing on well-known approaches concerning data presentation.

7
Presenting Data to the User

One of the most visible parts of an application is, for obvious reasons, the presentation of data to the user. Whether an application has a graphical interface or it provides a command line interface, the management of interaction between the user and the data managed by the application is always a critical aspect. Allowing the user to change data consistently and providing a feedback and/or a result often involves complex processing that can lead to code not always clear and difficult to maintain.

Some well-known patterns can help us design a structured code with many benefits in flexibility and maintainability. This chapter will focus on these patterns, known as **presentation patterns**, whose main goal is to separate presentation from data model. In particular, we will explore the three most known presentation patterns:

- Model-View-Controller pattern
- Model-View-Presenter pattern
- Model-View-ViewModel pattern

Managing user interfaces

One of the biggest problems in the development of any application is the interaction with the user. In whatever way the user interacts with the application, the code almost always ends up being complex and difficult to maintain. This is true for graphical interfaces and for command line consoles.

The user interface problems

The main reason for this complexity lies in the management of three aspects of the interaction between the user and the application: the **state**, the **logic**, and the **synchronization**.

The **state** is the set of information that represents the current picture of the user interface. It determines what the user sees at a given time and how it can interact with the application.

The **logic** is the set of operations that can be done on the elements of an interface in order to show or hide data or to make validation. It may be very complex depending on the type of processing to be performed on the data presented to the user.

The **synchronization** concerns those activities that map data shown to the user with data represented by the business objects managed by the application.

The combination of these elements creates most of the complexity in the presentation of data to the user and the interaction with the application.

User interfaces and JavaScript

The user interaction problems are usually independent from the language used to develop the application, so even for JavaScript applications we need to address these issues.

As we know, usually JavaScript is paired with HTML to create user interfaces. While HTML allows us to describe the graphical interface, JavaScript can manipulate its elements by adding logic, manipulating the state and managing the synchronization. JavaScript can access the HTML elements via the **Document Object Model** (**DOM**), an object-based representation of the user interface's markup.

Let's take a look at how a simple user interface is managed usually with HTML and JavaScript. Consider the following markup:

```
<label>Name <input type="text" id="txtName"></label><br/>
<label>Surname <input type="text" id="txtSurname"></label><br/>
<div id="divMessage"></div>

<button id="btnSave">Save</button>
<button id="btnReset">Reset</button>
```

It defines a simple form that allows entering the name and surname of a person and a button persist this data to storage. There is also an area intended to display any messages to the user. The graphical result of this HTML code is something similar to the following screenshot:

The following code is a typical example of how JavaScript can manage the user's interaction:

```
var person;
var txtName;
var txtSurname;
var btnSave;
var divMessage;

function Person(name, surname) {
  this.name = name;
  this.surname = surname;
}

function savePerson(person) {
  //Persist data or send it to a server
  console.log("Saved!");
}

window.onload = function() {
  txtName = document.getElementById("txtName");
  txtSurname = document.getElementById("txtSurname");
  btnSave = document.getElementById("btnSave");
  btnReset = document.getElementById("btnReset");
  divMessage = document.getElementById("divMessage");


  person = new Person("John", "Smith");

  txtName.value = person.name;
  txtSurname.value = person.surname;

  btnSave.onclick = function() {
    if (txtName.value && txtSurname.value) {
      person.name = txtName.value;
```

```
        person.surname = txtSurname.value;

        savePerson(person);
        divMessage.innerHTML = "Saved!";
      } else {
        divMessage.innerHTML = "Please, enter name and surname!";
      }
    };

    btnReset.onclick = function() {
      txtName.value = "";
      txtSurname.value = "";
      divMessage.innerHTML = "";

      person.name = "";
      person.surname = "";
    };
  };
```

We defined some global variables, the `Person()` constructor function for our business object and a `savePerson()` function that will make some processing in order to persist the data. Then, we attached some logic to the load event of the browser's current window. This logic allows displaying in the textboxes the current values of the properties of person object and manages the user's interaction with the **Save** and **Reset** buttons. The **Save** button calls the `savePerson()` function if data inserted by the user are valid, otherwise it displays a message requesting the user to enter the missing data. The **Reset** button clears the current content of the textboxes.

This code is fully functional, but its flexibility and its maintainability are not the best. There is a tight relationship between state, logic, and synchronization, so tight that even a seemingly small change can be a problem. What happens if we need to change the interface elements, for example, if we no longer want to display the message on a div but we want to display it in a textarea? What happens if we want to bring all the business logic and synchronization in another user interface, such as a command line interface?

Probably a lot of code should be adapted, and it might not be easy, despite the simplicity of the example. In this case, the **presentation patterns** can help us.

Presentation patterns

The **presentation patterns** are a category of design patterns specialized in presenting data to the user. They are widely used in the development of user interfaces and their basic principle is the separation of concerns. State, logic, and synchronization management are distributed among components that contribute to create a specific architecture promoting flexibility and maintainability. The idea behind separation of concerns in the presentation patterns is to make a clear division between business objects, that are objects that describe the real world, and presentation objects, that are the GUI elements we see on the screen. Business objects should be completely self-contained and work without reference to the presentation. They should also be able to support multiple presentations, possibly simultaneously, like, for example, both graphical and command-line interface.

Model, View, and Controller

Traditionally, a presentation pattern relies on three components.

The first component is the **Model**, which are the business objects that contain the information to be presented to the user. The model can be obtained from a service or is persisted in a database. It does not know anything about the way its information will be presented to the user and does not contain any logic. It is just data.

The **View** is the component responsible for displaying the data to the user and for catching user's interaction. It composes the user interface and represents the current state of the model. In a Web application, the view usually corresponds to the HTML markup that describes to the user the current model and allows

interactions. The third component can assume different names and roles, depending on the specific pattern. For example, it can be a **Controller**, **Presenter**, or **ViewModel**, as in the most known presentation patterns. This component usually contains the logic of the presentation architecture and may coordinate the information flow between the View and Model. In other words, it contributes to the synchronization between the current state and the underlying data model.

In the following sections, we will discuss the three most known presentation patterns: **Model-View-Controller** (**MVC**), **Model-View-Presenter** (**MVP**), and the **Model-View-ViewModel** (**MVVM**). These patterns and their variants are often referred to by **MV***, indicating that the constant parts of the patterns are the Model and View, although with different responsibilities. We will explore how they implement separation of concerns and implement the same example seen above by following the design principles of the three patterns.

The presentation patterns discussed in this chapter were not included in the GoF patterns. They are usually considered compound patterns that are patterns that can be built by composing other patterns. For example, View and Controller have strategy implementation, View itself can be a composite implementation, and View and Model can be synched through the observer pattern. Due to their wide spread, we will discuss them as if were not compound patterns.

The Model-View-Controller pattern

The Model-View-Controller pattern or **MVC** is one of the first presentation patterns designed in the 70s for the development of graphical user interfaces. Over the years, there have been several variants of the pattern, also due to the evolution of technology, but its basic structure remained virtually the same. As its name suggests, in addition to the Model and the View, the distinguishing feature is given by the Controller.

The Model, View, and Controller each have their own role and all together manage the user interaction, as depicted in the following image:

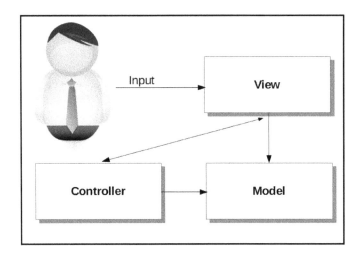

The View's role is to dealing with user's interaction. It displays the data provided by the Model and gets the user's input. The Controller interacts with the Model as the result of responding to the user input. When the user enters data through the view, the Controller intercepts the user's input and updates the Model. The distribution of tasks between the three components of the pattern promotes the creation of a more flexible and maintainable code.

To make the pattern's description more concrete, let's rewrite the code of the previous section by following the MVC architecture. As first step let's define the model:

```
var Model = (function () {
  function Model(name, surname) {
    this.name = name;
    this.surname = surname;
  }
  return Model;
}());
```

This constructor defines a person as Model with `name` and `surname` properties. Of course the Model can be defined as a class, as in the following:

```
class Model {
  constructor(name, surname) {
    this.name = name;
    this.surname = surname;
  }
}
```

Our View will manage the interaction with the user and the visualization of the Model data. The following code shows its implementation:

```
var View = (function () {
  function View(model, controller) {
    var self = this;
    var txtName = document.getElementById("txtName");
    var txtSurname = document.getElementById("txtSurname");
    var btnSave = document.getElementById("btnSave");
    var btnReset = document.getElementById("btnReset");

    self.controller = controller;
    txtName.value = model.name;
    txtSurname.value = model.surname;

    btnSave.onclick = function () {
      self.save();
    };

    btnReset.onclick = function () {
      self.clear();
    };
  }

  View.prototype.clear = function () {
    var txtName = document.getElementById("txtName");
    var txtSurname = document.getElementById("txtSurname");
```

```
      var divMessage = document.getElementById("divMessage");

      txtName.value = "";
      txtSurname.value = "";
      divMessage.innerHTML = "";
    };

    View.prototype.save = function () {
      var txtName = document.getElementById("txtName");
      var txtSurname = document.getElementById("txtSurname");
      var data = {
        name: txtName.value,
        surname: txtSurname.value
      };

      this.controller.save(data);
    };

    Object.defineProperty(View.prototype, "message", {
      set: function (message) {
        var divMessage = document.getElementById("divMessage");
        divMessage.innerHTML = message;
      },
      enumerable: true,
      configurable: true
    });

    return View;
  }());
```

As we can see, the constructor takes the `Model` and the `constructor` as arguments. It accesses the web page's elements through the DOM and maps the Model's values to them. The `clear()` and `save()` methods are attached to the constructor and are bound to the click event of the two buttons. The `clear()` method resets the textboxes of the web interfaces and the `save()` method gets the current values of the textboxes and passes them to the `save()` method of the Controller. Finally, the `message` property is attached to the View; it is mapped to the div reserved to display messages.

Again, we can define the View using the class syntax:

```
    class View {
      constructor(model, controller) {
        var self = this;
        var txtName = document.getElementById("txtName");
        var txtSurname = document.getElementById("txtSurname");
        var btnSave = document.getElementById("btnSave");
        var btnReset = document.getElementById("btnReset");
```

```
    self.controller = controller;

    txtName.value = model.name;
    txtSurname.value = model.surname;

    btnSave.onclick = function() {
      self.save();
    };

    btnReset.onclick =  function() {
      self.clear();
    };
  }

  clear() {
    var txtName = document.getElementById("txtName");
    var txtSurname = document.getElementById("txtSurname");
    var divMessage = document.getElementById("divMessage");


    txtName.value = "";
    txtSurname.value = "";
    divMessage.innerHTML = "";
  }

  set message(message) {
    var divMessage = document.getElementById("divMessage");

    divMessage.innerHTML = message;
  }

  save() {
    var txtName = document.getElementById("txtName");
    var txtSurname = document.getElementById("txtSurname");

    var data = {
      name: txtName.value,
      surname: txtSurname.value
    };

    this.controller.save(data);
  }
}
```

The `Controller()` constructor defines the `initialize()` method that sets a reference to the Model and the View. It also defines the `save()` method that makes a simple validation and updates the Model. The `save()` method also updates the View with an appropriate message:

```
var Controller = (function () {
  function Controller() {
  }

  Controller.prototype.initialize = function (model, view) {
    this.model = model;
    this.view = view;
  };

  Controller.prototype.save = function (data) {
    if (data.name && data.surname) {
      this.model.name = data.name;
      this.model.surname = data.surname;

      this.view.message = "Saved!";
    } else {
      this.view.message = "Please, enter name and surname!";
    }
  };

  return Controller;
}());
```

The following is the corresponding definition of the Controller as a class:

```
class Controller {
  initialize(model, view) {
    this.model = model;
    this.view = view;
  }

  save(data) {
    if (data.name && data.surname) {
      this.model.name = data.name;
      this.model.surname = data.surname;

      this.view.message = "Saved!";
    } else {
      this.view.message = "Please, enter name and surname!";
    }
  }
}
```

Once the three components of the Model-View-Controller pattern are defined, we have to compose them and start their cooperation. With this goal, we attach the following function to the load event of the browser's window:

```
window.onload = function() {
  var model = new Model("John", "Smith");
  var controller = new Controller();
  var view = new View(model, controller);

  controller.initialize(model, view);
};
```

The function creates a new Model and a new Controller. Then, it creates a View with the Model and Controller, passes it to the constructor, and finally calls the `initialize()` method of the Controller.

The code rewriting of this example maintains the same behavior seen earlier, but it reorganizes the code so that it can be easier to change it ad adapt it to new scenarios.

For example, if we decide to substitute the div displaying the message with a textarea, the only component that needs to be changed is the view. The other components remain unchanged and are unaware of the change. The same happens if we completely change the user interface, for instance, if we change the web page with a command line interface. In this case, we have to write a new View, but we do not need to change anything in the Model and in the Controller.

If we need to change the validation criteria of the user's input, we have to only change the Controller's code.

The code structuring provided by the MVC pattern allows us to easily locate the component to be modified based on the type of change.

The Model-View-Presenter pattern

The Model-View-Controller pattern gives us a better architecture for presenting data to the user. It assigns a specific task to each component so that possible changes might only concern one component letting the others unchanged. However, the three components of the MVC pattern remain someway interconnected: the View knows its Controller and the Model, and the Controller depends on the View and the Model. For example, a change to the Model may require changes to both the View and the Controller.

The Model-View-Presenter pattern or **MVP** proposes a layered architecture with fewer dependencies. In this pattern, the View intercepts the user interactions and asks the Presenter for changes to the Model. This means that the View does not directly interact with the Model, but acts on it through the Presenter. This eliminates any dependency between the View and the Model. The following image summarizes the pattern's architecture:

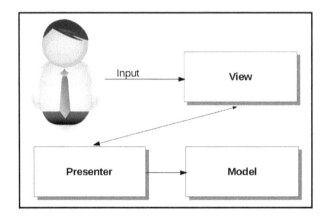

Let's look at how we can implement our reference example according to the MVP pattern.

The Model implementation remains the same as per the MVC pattern implementation.

Instead the View implementation is slightly different, as shown by the following code:

```
var View = (function () {
  function View(presenter) {
    var self = this;
    var btnSave = document.getElementById("btnSave");
    var btnReset = document.getElementById("btnReset");

    self.presenter = presenter;

    btnSave.onclick = function () {
      self.save();
    };

    btnReset.onclick = function () {
      self.clear();
    };
  }

  View.prototype.clear = function () {
    var txtName = document.getElementById("txtName");
```

```
      var txtSurname = document.getElementById("txtSurname");
      var divMessage = document.getElementById("divMessage");

      txtName.value = "";
      txtSurname.value = "";
      divMessage.innerHTML = "";
    };

    Object.defineProperty(View.prototype, "message", {
      set: function (message) {
        var divMessage = document.getElementById("divMessage");
        divMessage.innerHTML = message;
      }
    });

    Object.defineProperty(View.prototype, "name", {
      set: function (value) {
        var txtName = document.getElementById("txtName");
        txtName.value = value;
      }
    });

    Object.defineProperty(View.prototype, "surname", {
      set: function (value) {
        var txtSurname = document.getElementById("txtSurname");
        txtSurname.value = value;
      },
      enumerable: true,
      configurable: true
    });
    View.prototype.save = function () {
      var txtName = document.getElementById("txtName");
      var txtSurname = document.getElementById("txtSurname");
      var data = {
        name: txtName.value,
        surname: txtSurname.value
      };

      this.presenter.save(data);
    };
    return View;
  }());
```

The main difference with respect to the implementation of the MVC View is the definition of the `name` and `surname` properties. These properties are introduced in order to break the dependency between the View and the Model. Since the View does not know the Model, it exposes those properties which the Presenter will bind to the Model.

We can implement the View as a class as shown here:

```
class View {
  constructor(presenter) {
    var self = this;
    var btnSave = document.getElementById("btnSave");
    var btnReset = document.getElementById("btnReset");

    self.presenter = presenter;

    btnSave.onclick = function() {
      self.save();
    };
    btnReset.onclick =  function() {
      self.clear();
    };
  }

  clear() {
    var txtName = document.getElementById("txtName");
    var txtSurname = document.getElementById("txtSurname");
    var divMessage = document.getElementById("divMessage");

    txtName.value = "";
    txtSurname.value = "";
    divMessage.innerHTML = "";
  }

  set message(message) {
    var divMessage = document.getElementById("divMessage");
    divMessage.innerHTML = message;
  }

  set name(value) {
    var txtName = document.getElementById("txtName");
    txtName.value = value;
  }

  set surname(value) {
    var txtSurname = document.getElementById("txtSurname");
    txtSurname.value = value;
  }

  save() {
    var txtName = document.getElementById("txtName");
    var txtSurname = document.getElementById("txtSurname");

    var data = {
```

```
      name: txtName.value,
      surname: txtSurname.value
    };

    this.presenter.save(data);
  }
}
```

The Presenter's implementation is quite similar to the Controller's implementation in MVC pattern. The only difference to the MVC case is the assignments of the Model values to the properties of the View, as highlighted in the following code:

```
var Presenter = (function () {
  function Presenter() {
  }

  Presenter.prototype.initialize = function (model, view) {
    this.model = model;
    this.view = view;
    this.view.name = this.model.name;    this.view.surname =
    this.model.surname;
  };

  Presenter.prototype.save = function (data) {
    if (data.name && data.surname) {
      this.model.name = data.name;
      this.model.surname = data.surname;
      this.view.message = "Saved!";
    }
    else {
      this.view.message = "Please, enter name and surname!";
    }
  };

  return Presenter;
}());
```

The class version of the Presenter may be implemented as follows:

```
class Presenter {
  initialize(model,view) {
    this.model = model;
    this.view = view;

    this.view.name = this.model.name;
    this.view.surname = this.model.surname;
  }
```

```
save(data) {
  if (data.name && data.surname) {
    this.model.name = data.name;
    this.model.surname = data.surname;

    this.view.message = "Saved!";
  } else {
    this.view.message = "Please, enter name and surname!";
  }
}
}
```

Now, we can set up the pattern by creating the instances of the components as in the following code:

```
window.onload = function() {
  var model = new Model("John", "Smith");
  var presenter = new Presenter();
  var view = new View(presenter);

  presenter.initialize(model, view);
};
```

The MVP approach goes a step further in the separation of concerns among the three components of the pattern. Here, only the Presenter knows about the existence of both the Model and the View. This allows changes to the Model that does not require changes to the View. Only the Presenter has the responsibility to maintain the synchronization between the View and the Model.

 As for the other presentation patterns, even the MVP pattern has some implementation variants. In the real world, some prefer keeping basic logic still inside the View and taking complex logic in the Presenter, while others prefer keeping the entire logic in the Presenter. This leads to at least two subpatterns: the **MVP pattern with passive view**, where the logic included into the View is reduced to the minimum, and the **Supervising Controller pattern**, where some logic concerning simple declarative behavior is left inside the View.

The Model-View-ViewModel pattern

The Model-View-ViewModel pattern or **MVVM** tries to go further in reducing the dependencies among the presentation pattern components. This pattern introduces the **ViewModel** component that substitutes the Presenter. Of course, it is more than a simple renaming. Let's try to understand how it works by comparing it to the MVP pattern.

Just like with MVP, the View is totally unaware of the existence of the Model. But while in the MVP pattern, the View was aware that it was talking to some intermediate component. In the MVVM pattern, the View believes that the ViewModel is its Model. Instead of asking the Presenter to bind data and manipulate the Model, the View manages its own Model represented by the ViewModel. It acts as a wrapper around the actual Model and makes some consistency validations and other activities concerning the management of data.

The following image outlines the interactions between the components of the MVVM pattern:

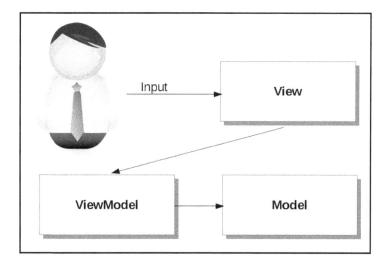

Let's take a look at how we can implement a View in the MVVM pattern:

```
var View = (function () {
  function View(modelView) {
    var self = this;
    var txtName = document.getElementById("txtName");
    var txtSurname = document.getElementById("txtSurname");
    var btnSave = document.getElementById("btnSave");
    var btnReset = document.getElementById("btnReset");
```

```
    self.modelView = modelView;
    txtName.value = modelView.name;
    txtSurname.value = modelView.surname;

    btnSave.onclick = function () {
      self.save();
    };

    btnReset.onclick = function () {
      self.clear();
    };
  }

View.prototype.clear = function () {
  var txtName = document.getElementById("txtName");
  var txtSurname = document.getElementById("txtSurname");
  var divMessage = document.getElementById("divMessage");

  txtName.value = "";
  txtSurname.value = "";
  divMessage.innerHTML = "";
};

View.prototype.setMessage = function (message) {
  var divMessage = document.getElementById("divMessage");
  divMessage.innerHTML = message;
};

View.prototype.save = function () {
  var txtName = document.getElementById("txtName");
  var txtSurname = document.getElementById("txtSurname");
  var data = {
    name: txtName.value,
    surname: txtSurname.value
  };

  this.modelView.save(data, this.setMessage);
};
  return View;
}());
```

As we can see from the preceding code, the View uses the ViewModel passed in the constructor as if it was the actual Model. It binds the ViewModel's properties to the elements of the user's interface and uses the ViewModel's methods to manipulate it.

The following code defines the View as a class:

```
class View {
  constructor(modelView) {
    var self = this;
    var txtName = document.getElementById("txtName");
    var txtSurname = document.getElementById("txtSurname");
    var btnSave = document.getElementById("btnSave");
    var btnReset = document.getElementById("btnReset");

    self.modelView = modelView;

    txtName.value = modelView.name;
    txtSurname.value = modelView.surname;

    btnSave.onclick = function() {
      self.save();
    };
    btnReset.onclick =  function() {
      self.clear();
    };
  }

  clear() {
    var txtName = document.getElementById("txtName");
    var txtSurname = document.getElementById("txtSurname");
    var divMessage = document.getElementById("divMessage");

    txtName.value = "";
    txtSurname.value = "";
    divMessage.innerHTML = "";
  }

  setMessage(message) {
    var divMessage = document.getElementById("divMessage");
    divMessage.innerHTML = message;
  }

  save() {
    var txtName = document.getElementById("txtName");
    var txtSurname = document.getElementById("txtSurname");

    var data = {
      name: txtName.value,
```

```
      surname: txtSurname.value
    };

    this.modelView.save(data, this.setMessage);
  }
}
```

As said before, the ViewModel wraps the Model and adds some methods to allow controlled data manipulation. The following code shows how we can implement it for our example:

```
var ViewModel = (function () {
  function ViewModel(model) {
    this.model = model;
  }

  Object.defineProperty(ViewModel.prototype, "name", {
    get: function () {
      return this.model.name;
    }
  });

  Object.defineProperty(ViewModel.prototype, "surname", {
    get: function () {
      return this.model.surname;
    }
  });

  ViewModel.prototype.save = function (data, callback) {
    if (data.name && data.surname) {
      this.model.name = data.name;
      this.model.surname = data.surname;

      if (callback) {
        callback("Saved!");
      }
    }
    else {
      if (callback) {
        callback("Please, enter name and surname!");
      }
    }
  };

  return ViewModel;
}());
```

The ViewModel definition exposes the `name` and `surname` properties of the underlying Model via its own read-only properties. Moreover, it defines the `save()` method that allows to update the Model after data validation. An interesting point in the `save()` method is the presence of the `callback` argument. This argument allows the caller to pass a function that will be called after the Model updating with information about the outcome of the operation. In our case, the ViewModel passes the message to be displayed as a parameter of the callback function. The use of the callback function allows to make the ViewModel independent from the View. Of course other techniques could be used, such as making the `save()` method to return the message or, even better, return code. The goal is to make the ViewModel unaware of the View using it.

We can define the ViewModel as a class with the following code:

```
class ViewModel {
  constructor(model) {
    this.model = model;
  }

  get name() {
    return this.model.name;
  }
  get surname() {
    return this.model.surname;
  }

  save(data, callback) {
    if (data.name && data.surname) {
      this.model.name = data.name;
      this.model.surname = data.surname;

      if (callback) {
        callback("Saved!");
      }

    } else {
      if (callback) {
        callback("Please, enter name and surname!");
      }
    }
  }
}
```

Now, we can combine all the components of the MVVM pattern to make them work:

```
window.onload = function() {
    var model = new Model("John", "Smith");
    var viewModel = new ViewModel(model);
    var view = new View(viewModel);
};
```

With this code, we created each component injecting in its constructor the only component it depends on.

A MV* pattern comparison

The three presentation patterns we have seen have many similarities. All them are based on three components, and the interactions between them are quite similar. However, each pattern has its own features that make it more suitable for certain situations and not for others. Let's recap the characteristics of each pattern highlighting those that stand out from each other.

The MVC pattern proposes cooperation among the three components Model, View, and Controller. Each component has its own role, but each one has some interactions with the other. The View uses the Model for initial binding, while the Controller manages the requests of changing the Model and gives feedbacks to the View. It is a first attempt to make separation of concerns, but some changes in one component may require arrangements in the others. After all, the MVC pattern is historically the oldest presentation pattern. Its origins date back to the 70s, when the first graphical user interfaces were very rudimentary.

The MVP pattern breaks the dependency between the View and the Model, entrusting to the Presenter to act as an intermediary. The View remains the only component responsible for managing the interaction with the user, while the Presenter is the only component authorized to manage the Model and to respond to the View. This architecture grants more independency among the components by introducing a layered structure.

The MVVM pattern goes further by assigning it to the intermediary component, the ViewModel, the role of a specialized model for the View. It interacts with the user and directly maps data to what it thinks to be the Model. In reality, this model is a wrapper around the underlying Model and its name, ViewModel, indicates that it represents the model for the View. As for the MVP pattern, this architecture is also layered, but each component depends only on the component that stays right below it. So, the View depends on the ViewModel, but not vice versa. The application of the MVVM pattern requires that the View has some capabilities to bind data and to implement some logic. This is the reason it is best suited to platforms which support bi-directional binding and have graphic elements with advanced built-in capabilities.

In conclusion, the MVC pattern assigns specific roles to each component, but does not care about coupling. The View and the Controller can interact with each other and the Model. This approach can be efficient from a performance point of view but may incur in security issues, since the entire Model is exposed to the View.

The MVP pattern makes the Model less vulnerable since it can be accessed just through the Presenter, but the Presenter layer itself may raise performance issues in complex applications.

The same considerations about the performance issues are valid for MVVM pattern, where a bit of logic is moved from the intermediary layer to the View layer.

Summary

In this chapter, we discussed how we can present data to the user from an object model perspective. We have seen how an unstructured approach leads to some problems in extensibility and maintainability of the code. The presentation patterns can help us better organize our code in order to design a flexible and clear architecture. The most known presentation patterns discussed in this chapter define three components that work together to achieve this goal.

We started by exploring the Mode-View-Controller pattern, whose components have a clear role and cooperate to manage the interactions between the user and the underlying data model. Then, we illustrated the Model-View-Presenter pattern, a pattern derived from MVC whose main difference is the introduction of a layered system. In fact, this pattern prevents a View to directly access the Model. This access is always mediated by the Presenter. Finally, we analyzed the View-Model-ModelView pattern, which maintains the layered approach of MVP and adds a new way to interpreting the role of the intermediary component between the View and the Model. This component is a specialized model for the view—the ViewModel. A comparison among the three patterns closed the chapter.

In the next chapter, we will explore a topic bound in someway to the presentation patterns. We will discuss the approaches to data binding and synchronization completing and improving the way we can present data to the user.

8
Data Binding

Data binding is one of the most appealing features in any programming environment. The capability to automatically update the property of an object bound to another one has a powerful charm, and many JavaScript frameworks and libraries support these features in different ways. In this chapter, we will discuss what data binding is and will describe some approaches to implement it in JavaScript applications without using any frameworks. The following topics will be discussed:

- Introduction to data binding
- Basic data binding implementation
- Observer and publish/subscribe patterns
- Using proxies for data binding implementation

What is data binding?

In general terms, **data binding** is a way to bind data to one or more objects ensuring synchronization. For example, associating a model to a view or simply assigning the value of an object's property to another object's property by granting synchronization are forms of data binding. Usually, data binding is related to the mapping between a model and a user interface, but in general it may concern any synchronized mapping between objects.

Data binding elements

In order to establish a data binding relationship between two objects, we need to define the following elements:

- **Data source object**: This is the object that represents the data to be bound, for example, the Model in an MV* context
- **Data source property**: This is the property of the data source object that actually contains the data we want to bind
- **Data target object**: This is the object we want associate the data to, typically the View in an MV* context
- **Data target property**: This is the property of the data target object that actually is the recipient of the data to bind
- **Synchronization mechanism**: This is the specific approach that allows us to assign the value of the data source property to the data target property and keeps the two properties updated

The following diagram shows how the data binding elements are related each other:

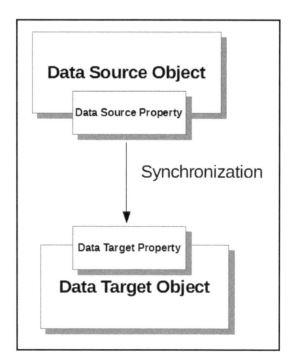

It is important to point out that the synchronization mechanism must update the data target property when a change to the data source property occurs. Its task is not a simple initial assignment of the two properties, but a constant alignment between the values of the two properties.

Data binding directions

Besides the involved elements, an important feature in a data binding relationship is its direction, which is the data flow of a binding action. When we described the elements of the relationship, we implicitly set a direction from the data source property to the data target property. This means that the value of the data source property determines the value of the data target property, and any change on the data source property must be reflected on the Data Target Property, not conversely. This is usually called **one-way data binding**.

One-way data binding can be useful, for example, when we want to display some data on the screen and want that any changes on these data will be immediately updated on the screen.

A special case of one-way data binding is when a change on the data target property updates the data source property. It is the opposite behavior described for one-way data binding. Actually, it is still one-way data binding, but the synchronization mechanism is reversed; the data source property provides the initial value to the data target property, but a change on the data target property determines the new value of the data source property. We will call it **reverse one-way data binding**.

A typical context where reverse one-way data binding occurs is when we display the value of an object's property in a text box. Usually in this context, we want that any changes on the textbox updates the object's property.

We can define a reverse relationship between the actors of a data binding relationship by swapping their roles. A data source object and its data source property become the data target object and data target property and vice versa. The two relationships are seen as one by calling it **two-way data binding**. In this context, the synchronization mechanism must grant that when the value of any property involved in the data binding relationship changes the other property must be updated consistently.

Implementing data binding

After clarifying what we mean by data binding, let's see what are the most common techniques used for its implementation. We will explore these techniques gradually going from the most simple to the most sophisticated that use advanced features of JavaScript.

Manual data binding

The simplest way to set up a data binding relationship between two objects is manual binding. Let's consider the following markup:

```
<label>Name <input type="text" id="txtName"></label><br/>
<label>Surname <input type="text" id="txtSurname"></label><br/>
<button id="btnSave">Save</button>
```

It defines an HTML view with two text boxes and a save button. In our data binding model, the DOM elements that correspond to the two textboxes are the data target objects. Now, let's consider the following code:

```
function Person(name, surname) {
  this.name = name;
  this.surname = surname;
}

person = new Person("John", "Smith");
```

The `person` object is the data source object for the data binding relationship we are trying to set up. The initial binding between the data source object and the data target object can be simply done by the following code:

```
var txtName = document.getElementById("txtName");
var txtSurname = document.getElementById("txtSurname");

txtName.value = person.name;
txtSurname.value = person.surname;
```

Now, we can define a reverse one-way data binding relationship using the click event on the save button, as shown here:

```
var btnSave = document.getElementById("btnSave");

btnSave.onclick = function() {
    person.name = txtName.value;
    person.surname = txtSurname.value;
};
```

With this approach, we defined a synchronization mechanism that updates the data source properties when the user changes data on the web page.

Monitoring changes

Even if rudimentary, this implementation is working and is widely used in contexts where there is no need for a more advanced solution. However, this approach could be not appropriate in some situations. In fact, the synchronization between the properties is not in real time, but it happens when the user clicks on the save button. This leaves the binding in an inconsistent state that can lead to unexpected behaviors. For example, an asynchronous or a scheduled task can access the data source properties when they are not yet updated. What we need is a sort of automatic data binding that updates the properties as soon as a new value is detected. In other words, we need to monitor when changes happen.

In order to apply real-time monitoring of changes, we can use the onchange event of the textboxes instead of onclick:

```
var txtName = document.getElementById("txtName");
var txtSurname = document.getElementById("txtSurname");

txtName.onchange = function() {
  person.name = txtName.value;
};

txtSurname.onchange = function() {
  person.surname = txtSurname.value;
};
```

This ensures that a change on any textbox is immediately reflected on the associated property.

However, this approach can be applied if the data target object supports events, as for DOM elements. How can we implement a real-time property update without events?

Suppose, for example, we want to create a two-way data binding between the textboxes and the properties of the person object, we need to complete the current binding by allowing the automatic update of textboxes when the properties of the person object change. However, we cannot rely on events, since our object does not support them.

A way around the problem is to define specialized methods to get and set values of the properties. Let's define a factory of the person object:

```
function createPerson(name, surname) {
  var _name = name;
  var _surname = surname;
  var txtName = document.getElementById("txtName");
  var txtSurname = document.getElementById("txtSurname");

  txtName.value = _name;
  txtSurname.value = _surname;

  return {
    name: function(value) {
      if (value) {
        _name = value;
        txtName.value = _name;
      }
      return _name;
    },
    surname: function(value) {
      if (value) {
        _surname = value;
        txtSurname.value = _surname;
      }
      return _name;
    }
  };
}
```

This function returns an object that has the `name()` and `surname()` methods instead of the `name` and `surname` properties. These methods work as getters when no argument is passed and as setters when an argument is passed. The following code shows how to use these methods:

```
person = createPerson("John", "Smith");
console.log(person.name());   //result: John

person.name("Mario");
console.log(person.name());   //result: Mario
```

If we look at the method's definition, we will find that in addition to managing the internal values of the properties, they map these values to the associated textboxes. This means that whenever a new value is assigned to the properties through these methods, it is automatically assigned to the bound textbox.

Adding the following code in the context of our example will update the textboxes after 5 seconds:

```
setTimeout(function() {
  person.name("Mario");
  person.surname("Rossi");
}, 5000);
```

In a real context, the data may be updated, for example, as a result of an Ajax call or by an asynchronous task.

Hacking properties

The previous proposed approach to monitoring changes of the data source properties is based on the definition of specialized getters and setters. That solution works properly also for old versions of JavaScript engines, but if we have no limitation on using more recent features, we can use the standard getters and setters using the `defineProperty()` method. So, let's define a constructor for the `Person` object as in the following code:

```
function Person(name, surname) {
  var _name = name;
  var _surname = surname;
  var txtName = document.getElementById("txtName");
  var txtSurname = document.getElementById("txtSurname");

  txtName.value = _name;
  txtSurname.value = _surname;

  Object.defineProperty(this, "name",
  {
    get: function() { return _name; },
    set: function(value) {
      _name = value;
      txtName.value = _name;
    }
  });

  Object.defineProperty(this, "surname",
  {
    get: function() { return _surname; },
```

```
    set: function(value) {
      _surname = value;
      txtSurname.value = _surname;
    }
  });
}
```

Here we can see, we defined the `name` and `surname` properties in quite a similar way to the `name()` and `surname()` methods of the previous approach. However, in this case, we have the benefit of keeping the standard syntactical approach in accessing properties, as the following example shows:

```
var person = new Person("John", "Smith");

setTimeout(function() {
  person.name = "Mario";
  person.surname = "Rossi";
}, 5000);
```

Thanks to the standard getters and setters definition, once defined, the constructor of the `Person` object, the data binding relationship is totally transparent.

Defining a binder

The data binding implementations we analyzed are based on a tight coupling between the data source object and the data target object. Whether we define specialized methods or we use the standard getter and setter, we include in the data source object definition an explicit reference to the data target object. Usually, this is not desirable, because a change to one object may require a change to the other object. Moreover, what happens if we want to create a new data binding relationship with another object? We need to add a reference to the new object by adding a new dependency and this slowly leads to a messy code.

What we need is an external mechanism that sets up a data binding relationship. Let's implement this mechanism as an object like the following:

```
function Binder() {}

Binder.prototype.bindTo =
function(dataSourceObj, dataSourceProperty, dataTargetObj,
dataTargetProperty) {
  Object.defineProperty(dataSourceObj, dataSourceProperty, {
    get: function() { return dataTargetObj[dataTargetProperty];     }
  });
}
```

The `Binder()` constructor defines the `bindTo()` method that takes the four actors of the data binding context, creates the specified property of the data source object, and binds it to the specified data the target property. In this way, it defines a reverse one-way data binding relationship between the data source object and the data target object.

With this approach, we brought the code creating the data binding relationship out of the definition of the data source object. So, we can define the relationship using the `bindTo()` method:

```
var person = new Person("John", "Smith");
var txtName = document.getElementById("txtName");
var txtSurname = document.getElementById("txtSurname");
var btnSave = document.getElementById("btnSave");
var binder = new Binder()

binder.bindTo(person, "name", txtName, "value");
binder.bindTo(person, "surname", txtSurname, "value");
```

When a change occurs in the `txtName` or `txtSurname` textboxes, the new value will be assigned to the bound properties. Analyzing the property definition inside the `bindTo()` method, we can see that there is not an actual assignment. We defined it so that any attempt to read its value returns the value of target property. Anyway, the effect is the same as that of an actual assignment.

We may also notice that the property has been defined as read-only, since there is no setter. It should not be so strange, since the data binding direction we defined is reverse one-way. If we allow to change the data source property, we risk to get inconsistent situations, where the data source property has a value different from the data target property.

It is not so difficult to add a method to the `Binder()` constructor so that we can define a two-way data binding relationship. The following is such an example:

```
Binder.prototype.bindTwoWay =
  function(dataSourceObj, dataSourceProperty, dataTargetObj,
dataTargetProperty) {
    Object.defineProperty(dataSourceObj, dataSourceProperty, {
      get: function() { return dataTargetObj[dataTargetProperty];
      },
      set: function(newValue) {dataTargetObj[dataTargetProperty]
      = newValue; }
    });
  }
```

As we can see, we simply added a setter to the data source property definition that assigns the new value to the data target property. This simple addition makes the two properties tightly synchronized, since the actual value is kept by the data target property and the data source property act as its wrapper.

Even if this solution is very effective, it has some issues. Since it redefines a possible existing property, we risk losing the original definition which may have a customized behavior. Moreover, the properties involved in the data binding relationship may be sealed so that we cannot change its definition. This happens, for example, with the DOM elements. We can't change the DOM's elements definition, so if we plan to use the `bindTwoWay()` method on a DOM element we will fail.

The publish/subscribe pattern

We will try to overcome the limitations of previous data binding implementations by using a design pattern. We can choose to apply the **observer pattern** or **publisher/subscriber pattern**. Both are intended to manage a scenario where one or more objects are interested in receiving notifications when the state of another object changes. The solutions proposed by the patterns are similar and often the two patterns are confused or considered as two different names for the same pattern. Actually, there are important differences, as we will see in the following sections.

The observer pattern

The observer pattern is maybe widely known because it is included in the patterns proposed by the Gang of Four. In its simplified version for JavaScript, that is, not considering class abstractions, it involves the following actors:

- **Subject**: This is the object that may change its state; it knows its observer and sends them a notification when its state changes.
- **Observers**: These are the objects that are interested in the subject's state change.

An observer that wants to know when changes of the subject's state occur registers itself with the subject. The subject will notify a change of its state to all registered observers.

The following diagram describes graphically the interactions between the subject and the observers:

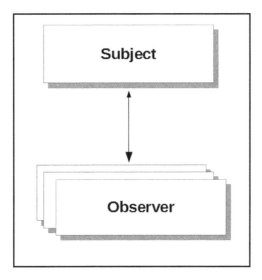

Simply put, the observer pattern proposes that the subject directly notifies its observers of its state changes. If we turn back to the data binding implementation we made so far, we can see that they applied an approach similar to this pattern. For example, when we used the onchange event to be notified if the value of the textbox changed, we were applying the observer pattern. In fact, the textbox was the subject and the person object was the observer.

Even when we used the getter and setter methods of a property, somehow, we applied this pattern; but in that case, we did not generate a notification, instead, directly updated the value of the observer's property.

The publisher/subscriber pattern

The publisher/subscriber pattern is a variant of the observer pattern, which introduces a third component in order to decouple the subject from the observersâ©©the **observable**.

While in the observer pattern, the subject itself manages the communication with its observers, in the publisher/subscriber pattern this task is assigned to the observable object. The following diagram shows this new scenario:

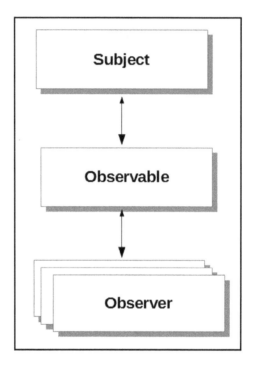

We will take this pattern as a reference to implement a new approach for data binding.

Implementing observables

Different from what we made so far, we will try to implement data binding introducing an intermediary object between the data source object and the data target object, as suggested by the publisher/subscriber pattern. Our intermediary object will be the observable object implemented by the following factory function:

```
function observable(value) {
    var subscribers = [];

    function notify(newValue) {
        for (var i = 0; i < subscribers.length; i++) {
            subscribers[i](newValue);
        }
```

```
      }

      function accessor(newValue) {
        if (arguments.length && newValue !== value) {
          value = newValue;
          notify(newValue);
        }
        return value;
      }

      accessor.subscribe = function(subscriber) {
        subscribers.push(subscriber);
      };

      return accessor;
    }
```

This function takes the subject as an argument, that is, the value to observe, and returns a function that represents its observable. The returned function acts as an accessor to the subject that manages subscriptions in order to notify the subject's changes.

We can see that the `observable()` function has a private array of subscribers, which is populated by the `subscribe()` method attached to the `accessor()` function. The `subscribers` array contains a list of functions to be executed when a change of the subject's status occurs. The `accessor()` function works as the specialized getter and setter seen in a previous implementation; when no argument is passed, it returns the current value of the subject, otherwise, it sets the current value of the subject with the passed one and notifies the change to all subscribers.

Let's rewrite our example using the `observable()` function and apply the publisher/subscriber pattern. The code will be as follows:

```
function Person(name, surname) {
  this.name = name;
  this.surname = surname;
}


var john = observable("John");
var smith = observable("Smith");
var txtName = document.getElementById("txtName");
var txtSurname = document.getElementById("txtSurname");

person = new Person(john, smith);

txtName.value = person.name();
```

```
txtSurname.value = person.surname()

person.name.subscribe( function(value) { txtName.value = value; });
person.surname.subscribe( function(value) { txtSurname.value = value; });

setTimeout(function() {
  person.name("Mario");
  person.surname("Rossi");
}, 5000);
```

Here, we can see that the `Person()` constructor is a plain constructor without any reference to its observers. We create two observables bound to the strings `"John"` and `"Smith"` and then create a `person` instance by passing the two observables as values for `name` and `surname` properties. Then, these observables subscribe a function that updates the associated textbox value when changes occur.

With this infrastructure, when the properties of the `person` object are changed, the observable will create a notification by executing the function associated with each subscriber. In our example, after 5 seconds a new name and surname are assigned to the `person` object.

 Each library or framework has its own approach in implementing data binding, for example, the implementation of data binding based on observables. Described in this section is the core of the Knockout library.

 AngularJS, another framework supporting advanced data binding, follows a different approach. It uses a global monitoring system based on the concept of watch. In short words, a watch observes a variable, and for each execution cycle, the framework checks if some associated value has changed and possibly updates the depending values.

The data binding implementing through the observables makes the data source object independent from the data target object. It is applicable to any type of object, including the DOM elements and is quite generic. In fact, we can execute an arbitrary code when the change occurs by subscribing any function, not just a simple assignment.

Using proxies

An alternative approach to implements data binding may be based on a new feature introduced by ECMAScript 6-**proxies**.

The proxy class

The **proxy** class allows us to create special objects that can change the default behavior when an object is accessed. When creating a proxy for an object, we can define a handler and configure **traps** in order to intercept accesses to its property and possibly change the standard behavior.

Let's explain the basic behavior of proxies with an example. Suppose we want to track to the console every access to the properties of an object. We can define the following handler:

```
var handler = {
  get (target, propertyName) {
    console.log("Getting property " + propertyName);
    return target[propertyName];
  },
  set(target, propertyName, value) {
    console.log("Assigning value " + value + " to property " +
    propertyName);
    target[propertyName] = value;
  }
};
```

This handler is an object with two methods, `get()` and `set()`, that intercept the getter and the setter of the target object. These methods are called traps and allow intercept accesses the target object. The getter writes on the console and returns the value of the target's property. The setter writes on the console and sets the passed value to the target's property. In this case, we want to keep the standard behavior of the target object, but in general, we can return or assign to the target's properties any value changing the default behavior.

Once we defined the handler, we can create a proxy for an object and assign the handler to it:

```
var person = new Person("John", "Smith");
var proxiedPerson = new Proxy(person, handler);
```

Now, each access to the `proxiedPerson` object will affect the `person` object and will log on the console:

```
var name = proxiedPerson.name;
//console: Getting property name

proxiedPerson.name = "Mario";
//console: Assigning value Mario to property name

console.log(person.name);
//console: Mario
```

Of course this is a simple example to introduce the basic concepts of proxies. We can use other traps in order to define advanced manipulations of the target object. For example, we can trap definitions of properties using the `defineProperty()` trap or deletion of properties using the trap `deleteProperty()` function and so on.

Data binding with proxies

We have seen how proxies can intercept accesses to the properties of an object in a transparent way. So, we will try to exploit it by implementing data binding.

Let's define a `Binder` class with a `bindTo()` method as in the following:

```
class Binder {
  bindTo(dataSourceObj, dataSourceProperty, dataTargetObj,
dataTargetProperty) {
    var bindHandler = {
      set: function(target, property, newValue) {
        if (property == dataSourceProperty) {
          target[dataSourceProperty] = newValue;

          dataTargetObj[dataTargetProperty] = newValue;
        }
      }
    };
    return new Proxy(dataSourceObj, bindHandler);
  }
}
```

The `bindTo()` method defines a setter trap for the data source object so that each change to the specified property `dataSourceProperty` updates the associated property of the data target object. The `bindTo()` method returns the proxy created on the data source object, so we can use it as in the following example:

```
var person = new Person("John", "Smith");
var txtName = document.getElementById("txtName");
var binder = new Binder();

var proxiedPerson = binder.bindTo(person, "name", txtName,   "value");

setTimeout(function() {
  proxiedPerson.name = "Mario";
}, 5000);
```

We created a proxied version of the `person` object using the `bindTo()` method by specifying the binding between the `name` property and the `value` property of the associated textbox. So each change on the name property of the `proxiedPerson` object reflects on both the `name` property of the `person` object and on the `value` property of the textbox.

This example takes into account only the property `name`. If we want also to consider the `surname` property, we need to create a new proxy via the `bindTo()` method. Instead of creating a proxy for each property we want to bind, we can extend the `bindTo()` method to take a list of properties of the data source object to bind and a list of pairs composed by the data target object and data target property. The following example shows the `Binder` class changed to support multiple bindings:

```
class Binder {
   bindTo(dataSourceObj, dataSourceProperties, dataTargetList) {
      var bindHandler = {
         set: function(target, property, newValue) {
            var i = dataSourceProperties.indexOf(property);

            if (i >= 0) {
               target[dataSourceProperties[i]] = newValue;

               dataTargetList[i].obj[dataTargetList[i].prop] =
               newValue;
            }
         }
      };
      return new Proxy(dataSourceObj, bindHandler);
   }
}
```

In this class, the `dataTargetList` argument is an array of objects with two properties: the `obj` property stores the data target object and the `prop` property contains the data target property.

Now, we can use this class as in the following code:

```
var person = new Person("John", "Smith");
var txtName = document.getElementById("txtName");
var txtSurname = document.getElementById("txtSurname");
var binder = new Binder();

var proxiedPerson = binder.bindTo(person,
                    ["name", "surname"],
                    [   {obj: txtName, prop: "value"},
                        {obj: txtSurname, prop: "value"}
                    ]);
```

In addition to the proxy object, one of the JavaScript features that generated interest in recent times is **Object.observe()**, also known as **O.o**. This method was intended to create a native Observer on an object and it should have been included in version 7 of ECMAScript. Some browsers such as Chrome and Opera already support it. However, the proposal has been withdrawn by the end of 2015, as announced by Adam Klein in his post at `https://esdiscuss.org/topic/an-update-on-object-observe`.

Summary

In this chapter, we introduced the basic concepts about data binding and the terminology used to indicate the various actors involved in the binding relationship. Then, we started exploring different ways to implement data binding in JavaScript. The simplest way was the manual implementation, which is the manual assignment of values from an object to another after an event generated by the user. We saw that a better implementation should monitor changes on the data source object and update in real time the data target object. We also tried to redefine the properties of an object in order to catch changes and synchronize the data target property, but found that this technique may have some issues.

Our exploration continued with the presentation of the observer pattern and the publisher/subscriber pattern. We used the latter to implement a solution based on observables. Finally, we introduced ECMAScript 6 proxies and described an approach based on them.

In the next chapter, we will discuss how to write asynchronous code and how to use Promises.

9

Asynchronous Programming and Promises

Asynchronous programming is a part of the nature of JavaScript since its birth. Regardless of the runtime environment of JavaScript, you cannot ignore the execution of asynchronous code, whether it is the management of user's interaction with a graphical interface or the interaction with a server or a hardware component of the system.

This chapter will discuss how to manage asynchronous code in JavaScript by analyzing the classical approach based on callback functions, pointing out its intrinsic drawbacks and exploring new approaches such as the ones based on Promises and Generators.

The following topics will be discussed in the chapter:

- Events and asynchronous calls
- Callback functions
- Troubles with callbacks
- ES6 Promises
- A Generator-based approach

Is JavaScript asynchronous?

In JavaScript programming, we often deal with activities virtually executed concurrently. For instance, events can occur independently from the main execution flow of an application and many events can occur at the same time. If we attached handlers for many events, we expect these to run immediately upon the occurrence of the associated event.

Actually, things are not exactly like that. JavaScript concurrency model is not really parallel or multithread. Even if events can occur in parallel, their handling is sequential and the interactions between the involved codes is asynchronous. This means that an event can occur at a given time, but the execution of its handler can occur after some time.

Event loop and asynchronous code

In languages that support concurrency, the code of a thread can be interrupted to take the code of another thread forward. In JavaScript, everything happens in one single thread. The concurrency model that gives the impression that many threads are executing is the **event loop**-each event inserts a message into a queue that will be sequentially processed by the JavaScript runtime in an endless loop.

Basically, the main task of a JavaScript engine is to check for messages in the queue and to run the code of event handlers before moving to the next message. It is important to understand that the code executed between a message and the next one is executed without any interruption. Any event that occurs during the execution of a cycle of the event loop can't stop it.

We can realize this behavior by doing some experiments with the timers. Consider, for example, the following code:

```
console.log("First");
setTimeout(function() { console.log("Second"); }, 300);
console.log("Third");
```

As we expect, the output of its execution is as follows:

```
First
Third
Second
```

What happens if we set the timeout interval to zero?

```
console.log("First");
setTimeout(function() { console.log("Second"); }, 0);
console.log("Third");
```

Maybe we would expect that the second statement is executed immediately. Instead, the output will be the same as before. Even if we set an empty timeout, the execution of `setTimeout()` puts a message in the message queue and cannot stop the execution of current code. So, the `Second` string will be sent to the console after the completion of current execution.

Events, Ajax, and other asynchronous stuff

Writing JavaScript applications we have many chances to write asynchronous code. In addition to timers, we usually write asynchronous code when we need to manage events, such as DOM events in a browser or when we need to interact with a server through Ajax. But, we deal with asynchronous programming also when handling server-sent event, when managing communication with web workers, when accessing a file system, and so on. Since JavaScript is increasingly spreading even outside the Web, the role of asynchronous programming is gaining growing importance. So, we need to understand how it works and what kind of problems the asynchronous code may raise.

Writing asynchronous code

Most of us have surely written asynchronous code without paying much attention. Actually, in simple situations we do not need to make great assumptions and our code follows the simplicity of the context. But when the complexity grows, writing, managing, and understanding the asynchronous code may become a messy business. Let's take a look at how we usually write asynchronous code and which issues may come out.

Using events properties

The most common situation where we write asynchronous code is when we need to manage events. Consider the interaction of the user with the GUIâ◎◎a click on a button activates the execution of a handler that we attached to it.

One of the ways to attach a handler to an event is using the event property. For example, an HTML button has an `onclick` property, we can attach our handler to:

```
var btn = document.getElementById("myBtn");
btn.onclick = function() {
  console.log("The button was clicked!");
};
```

When the click event occurs, the function attached to the `onclick` property is executed and the message appears on the console.

Another common example is when using Ajax to make HTTP requests to a remote server, as in the following example:

```
var httpReq = new XMLHttpRequest();

httpReq.onreadystatechange = function() {
  if (httpReq.readyState == 4 && httpReq.status == 200) {
    console.log(httpReq.responseText);
  }
};

httpReq.open("GET", "/myServerPage", true);
httpReq.send();
```

Here, we attached the event handler to the `onreadystatechange` property of the `XMLHttpRequest` object. Each time the `readyState` property of the `XMLHttpRequest` object changes, that is on each phase of client-server communication, the handler is executed. Just when a complete response is obtained from the server, we will show it on the console.

In both cases, the code is quite simple and it seems that no particular trouble may arise. We write code to be executed asynchronously by attaching it to specific properties that are hooks for events. The only difference in comparison to the usual coding is that the event handler is not explicitly called by our code, but it is called by the JavaScript runtime. So the execution flow of our code is not sequential, but it can have different flows based on the events that occur.

Using callbacks

Another and more common way to write asynchronous code is based on callback functions. A **callback function** or simply **callback** is a function passed as an argument to another function so that it will be invoked inside the latter. Usually, the callback function is executed when a specific event occurs, as in the following example:

```
var btn = document.getElementById("myBtn");

btn.addEventListener("click", function() {
  console.log("The button was clicked!");
});
```

This code has the same effect as the previous one, where we attached the event handler to the `onclick` property of the button. Here, we use the `addEventListener()` method of the button to attach a handler for the `click` event. Again, the only apparent effect in writing asynchronous code as a callback is a non-sequential execution flow, as in the previous case:

Callbacks and this

Attaching code to events properties or passing callbacks to be executed asynchronously seems to have no major impact on the overall code. However, it may give rise to some subtle issues. Consider the following code:

```
function myButton(id, standardText, clickedText) {
    this.id = id;
    this.standardText = standardText;
    this.clickedText = clickedText;

    var btn = document.getElementById(this.id);
    btn.innerHTML = this.standardText;

    btn.addEventListener("click", function(){
        btn.innerHTML= this.clickedText;
    });
}
```

It is a constructor function that transforms an HTML button into a custom button. The button has an initial text on it, and when the user clicks it, then the text changes. The code stores the parameters in properties and attaches a handler for the click event. We can use the constructor as in the following example:

```
var myBtn = new myButton("btn", "Click me!", "Clicked!");
```

At first glance it seems quite correct, but if we run the code we do not get the expected result. Instead of getting the `Clicked!` text on the button when we click it, we will get the `undefined` text. What happens here?

The unexpected behavior depends on the use of the `this` keyword within the click event handler:

```
btn.addEventListener("click", function(){
    btn.innerHTML= this.clickedText;
});
```

In fact, the value of the `this` keyword within a function only depends on how the function is called, not on how it is defined.

Since the handler runs asynchronously, the execution context will be different from the one of the main execution flow. So, the `this` keyword is not bound to the instance of the constructor, but to the current context. In our example, it will be bound to the window object of the browser, which has not a `clickedText` property.

We have a few ways to correctly manage the use of the `this` keyword inside asynchronous functions.

The first and most common approach is not using `this`. In most cases, we don't want to access the current context represented by the `this` key, but the object it refers to. So, we can catch it in a variable and use the variable instead of directly accessing `this`. Usually, the variable is named `self` or `that`, but of course it can have any name. The following code shows how to use this approach using the variable`self` instead of `this`:

```
function myButton(id, standardText, clickedText) {
  var self = this;

  self.id = id;
  self.standardText = standardText;
  self.clickedText = clickedText;

  var btn = document.getElementById(self.id);
  btn.innerHTML = self.standardText;

  btn.addEventListener("click", function(){
    btn.innerHTML= self.clickedText;
  });
}
```

In this case, the reference to `this` is already resolved when the asynchronous code of the event handler is executed and no ambiguity arises.

An alternative approach is to explicitly set the value of `this` keyword to the event handler. In fact, any function has the `bind()` method that allows to specify the value to assign to the `this` keyword when the function will be executed. The `bind()` method takes the value to assign to `this` and returns a function with the requested binding. If we want to apply this approach to our example, we will define our event handler as follows:

```
var clickHandler = (function(){
  btn.innerHTML= this.clickedText;
}).bind(this);

btn.addEventListener("click", clickHandler);
```

When the handler will be executed, the value of `this` will refer to the value it had during the function definition, that is, the constructor instance.

A third way to avoid ambiguity when using the `this` keyword in an asynchronous context is the use of arrow functions. ECMAScript 6 introduced **arrow functions** as anonymous functions with a more concise syntax and a lexical scope for the `this` keyword. In its basic form, an arrow function is an expression with a list of parameters in parentheses, a *fat arrow* symbol (=>) and a function body or an expression. For example, the following arrow function sets a value into a textbox:

```
(value) => { document.getElementById("txtText").value = value; }
```

The following example returns the sum of two numbers:

```
(a, b) => {return a + b;}
```

It is equivalent to the following expression:

```
(a, b) => a + b;
```

Using an arrow function, we can define our event handler as in the following:

```
function myButton(id, standardText, clickedText) {
  this.id = id;
  this.standardText = standardText;
  this.clickedText = clickedText;

  var btn = document.getElementById(this.id);
  btn.innerHTML = this.standardText;

  btn.addEventListener("click",
    () => { btn.innerHTML= this.clickedText; });
}
```

By design, the arrow function keeps the `this` keyword bound to the value it has at function definition time. So, we do not need to use the `bind()` method as in the previous example.

The callback hell

We have just seen how a quite simple code as an event handler may affect the meaning of the `this` keyword due to its asynchronous nature. A few measures can help us overcome the issue, but it is not the only potential problem with asynchronous code.

Let's introduce an example involving asynchronous HTTP calls submitted to a server. The following is the definition of a function that uses the XMLHttpRequest object to make an HTTP request and execute a callback function on data returned by the server:

```
function httpGet(url, callback) {
 var httpReq = new XMLHttpRequest();

  httpReq.onreadystatechange = function() {
    var data;

    if (httpReq.readyState == 4 && httpReq.status == 200) {
      data = JSON.parse(httpReq.responseText);
      callback(data);
    } else {
      throw new Error(httpReq.statusText);
    }
  };

  httpReq.open("GET", url, true);
  httpReq.send();
}
```

The function takes the URL of the web resource to the get and the callback function to execute when data are returned by the server. The code inside the body of the function is the standard HTTP request via XMLHttpRequest the asynchronous call made by the send() method is resumed when the onreadystatechange event occurs.

Let's consider the usage of this function in the following code:

```
httpGet("/users/12345",
  function(user) {
    httpGet("/blogs/" + user.blogId,
    function(blog) {
      displayPostList(blog.posts);
    });

    httpGet("/photos/" + user.albumId,
      function(album) {
        displayPhotoList(album.photos);
      }
    );
  }
);
```

It uses the `httpGet()` function to get a user's data. Once the data are received, the callback function makes two new requests to the server to get the user's blog and the user's photos. Again, when the server returns the requested data, they are displayed on the screen using the `displayPostList()` and `displayPhotoList()` functions.

Here, we have a single function call with some nested callbacks that make the code not very readable. The callback functions need to be nested since each call depends on the outcome of the previous nesting level. The requests of user's blog and photos cannot be made before getting the user's data. However, once we receive the user's data, we can request the user's blog and photos at the same time.

Displaying user's posts and photos is asynchronous and the photos will not necessarily be displayed after the posts. If we want to constrain the display order or make some processing based on both results before displaying them (for example, show only photos related to the posts), we should find a way to synchronize the callback functions, a task whose complexity we can easily guess.

Using callbacks in this way creates some issues both in code readability and asynchronous tasks synchronization. This is what the **callback hell** is commonly called.

Organizing callbacks

A first attempt to bring order to the code is to use named functions instead of anonymous functions. Let's rewrite the previous code as in the following example:

```
function getUserBlogAndPhoto(user) {
  getBlog(user.blogId);
  getPhotos(user.albumId);
}

function getBlog(blogId) {
  httpGet("/blogs/" + blogId, displayBlog);
}

function displayBlog(blog) {
  displayPostList(blog.posts);
}

function getPhotos(albumId) {
  httpGet("/photos/" + user.albumId,  displayAlbum);
}

function displayAlbum(album) {
  displayPhotoList(album.photos);
```

```
    }

    httpGet("/users/12345",  getUserBlogAndPhoto);
```

The code now appears less confused, but not clear enough. To understand what the code means we need to figure out the execution flow by following the callback function names passed to the `httpGet()` function. Anyway, even if using named functions as callbacks can help us make code a bit more readable, it does not solve the synchronization problem.

The issues of asynchronous code

Using callback functions can be quite intuitive in simple cases, but it can quickly turn into a nightmare when the code complexity increases.

The major flaws of the intensive use of callbacks include:

- Poor readability of the code, which soon may become affected by the so-called **pyramid of doom**; the expansion to the right due to the indiscriminate callback nesting and related indentation.
- Difficult composition of callbacks and synchronization of the processing flow; to try composition and synchronization it is often necessary to invent artifices that make the code even more unreadable and sometimes inefficient.
- Difficult error handling and debugging, especially in the presence of anonymous callback.

Let's consider the last point. What happens when an error occurs within a callback? Suppose we try to catch error as in the following example:

```
try {
  httpGet("/users/12345",
  function(user) {
    httpGet("/blogs/" + user.blogId,
    function(blog) {
      displayPostList(blog.posts);
    });

    httpGet("/photos/" + user.albumId,
      function(album) {
        displayPhotoList(album.photos);
      }
    );
  }
);
```

```
  } catch(e) {
    console.log("An error occurred: " e.message);
  }
```

Although it may seem like a possible solution to the untrained eye, the `try/catch` statements are completely useless in an asynchronous context. Since `httpGet()` calls involve asynchronous code, the `try` block is executed before any actual request is submitted to the server. So, the possible exception in the callbacks is out of the scope of the `try` statement.

In conclusion, unlike the synchronous calls to functions whose execution returns a value or exception, in the case of asynchronous calls, we do not have none of the two things. As a result there is less possibility of function composition and any exception handling. In short, with an asynchronous approach, we lose some of the typical features of the functional programming model that inspires JavaScript.

Introducing Promises

From the previous considerations, we can conclude that, despite their common usage, callback functions are not so suitable to manage asynchronous programming. They allow us to execute asynchronous code, but we have not a strong control on synchronization, error handling, and code readability.

In last years, an alternative pattern for managing asynchronous code is spreading in the JavaScript communityâ®®the Promise pattern.

What are Promises?

Promises are objects that represent a value that we can handle at some point in the future. They can be used to capture the outcome of an asynchronous activity, such as an event, and to manage it in a consistent way. In fact, unlike event handling, using callbacks, Promises guarantees us to receive a result, even if the event occurs before we register to handle it (in contrast to event that can incur in race conditions) and allow us to catch and handle exceptions. Moreover, they allow us to write code with a synchronous style gaining readability.

Promises have been around for a while and used by the JavaScript community in the form of libraries. They are defined by a specification called **Promise/A+** and implemented by libraries such as Q, When.js or RSVP.js, jQuery, and supported by frameworks such as AngularJS. Although the various Promise implementations follow the standardized behavior, their APIs have some differences.

 Various attempts have been made to define a common specification for Promises in JavaScript. The most known ones have been published by the CommonJS community with Promise/A, Promise/B, and an interoperable specification Promise/D. The specifications implemented by ECMAScript 6 is the Promise/A+ specifications and can be found at `https://promisesa plus.com/`.

Fortunately, ECMAScript 6 introduced Promises in JavaScript as native objects, so we can rely on a uniform API layer to manage asynchronous code, as we will see in the following sections.

The Promise terminology

Before seeing how to use Promises to manage asynchronous code, we have to introduce some terms we will use while talking about them. Let's start by illustrating the states that a Promise can have:

- **Resolved or fulfilled**: A Promise is resolved or fulfilled when the value it represents is available, that is, when the asynchronous task associated with it returns the requested value.
- **Rejected**: A Promise is rejected when the asynchronous task associated with it fails to return a value, maybe for an exception or because the returned value is not considered valid.
- **Pending**: This is the state of a Promise until it is not resolved or rejected, that is the request to start an asynchronous task has been made but we have not yet a result.

Usually, when a Promise has resolved or rejected, we say that it is **settled**.

Remember that a Promise can only be settled once and other consumers of a Promise cannot change its state; that is, a Promise is **immutable**.

Creating Promises

Once introduced to the Promise terminology, let's explore how we can create and use it to better to handle asynchronous code. We will analyze the ES6 Promise syntax, since it is a standard specification and hopefully all current libraries will disappear or comply within near future.

We can create a Promise using the `Promise()` constructor, as shown here:

```
var promise = new Promise(handler);
```

The `Promise()` constructor takes a function as an argument whose task is to manage the fulfillment or rejection of the Promise. Typically, a Promise handler has the following structure:

```
var promise = new Promise(function(resolve, reject) {
  if (condition)  {  //some condition
    resolve(value);  //successfully resolve the Promise
  } else {
    reject(reason);  //reject the Promise and specify the reason
  }
});
```

The Promise handler is given two functions as parameters.

The first parameter (`resolve` in the example) is the function to call when the value returned by the asynchronous task is available. The returned value is passed to the resolve function.

The second parameter (`reject` in the example) is the function to call if the Promise can't be resolved, for instance, because an error occurred or the value is not valid. When a Promise is rejected, a reason is passed to the reject function, such as an exception.

In order to show how to concretely create a Promise, let's rewrite the `httpGet()` function seen earlier:

```
function httpGet(url) {
  return new Promise(function(resolve, reject) {
    var httpReq = new XMLHttpRequest();

    httpReq.onreadystatechange = function() {
      var data;

      if (httpReq.readyState == 4) {
        if (httpReq.status == 200) {
          data = JSON.parse(httpReq.responseText);
```

```
        resolve(data);
      } else {
        reject(new Error(httpReq.statusText));
      }
    }
  };

  httpReq.open("GET", url, true);
  httpReq.send();
 });
}
```

This version of the `httpGet()` function takes just one argument: the `url` that should respond to our HTTP request. The function returns a Promise whose handler is quite similar to previous version of the `httpGet()` function. In fact, it creates an `XMLHttpRequest` object to make the HTTP request as usual, but it calls the `resolve()` function when it receives a successful response from the server; it calls the `reject()` function when it receives an unsuccessful response. In the first case, the response's content is passed to the `resolve()` function; in the second case, an exception with the HTTP status message is passed to the `reject()` function.

So, now the `httpGet()` function returns a Promise instead of directly submitting the HTTP request to the server.

Consuming Promises

Since a Promise is an object, it can be used as any other object; it can be stored in a variable, passed as a parameter, returned by a function and so on. For example, we can store the promise returned by the `httpGet()` function in a variable, as shown by the following code:

```
var myPromise = httpGet("/users/12345")
```

When we want to consume the Promise, that is, we want to process the value it represents, we need to use its `then()` method. We pass a function as a parameter to the `then()` method and this function will receive the Promise's value once it will be resolved.

Let's take a simplified version of the example seen earlier. We use the new Promise-based `httpGet()` function to get the user's data and access his blog. Our code will look like the following:

```
httpGet("/users/12345")
  .then(function(user) {
    console.log("The user's blog has the id " + user.blogId);
  });
```

As we can see, we pass a function to the `then()` method whose argument `user` will be bound to the data received from the server asynchronously. When the data will be available, the Promise is resolved and the function will be called.

In order to display the list of blog posts of the user, we will write the following code:

```
httpGet("/users/12345")
  .then(function(user) {
    httpGet("/blogs/" + user.blogId)
      .then(function(blog) {
        displayPostList(blog.posts);
      });
  });
```

Here, the function handling the resolved Promise creates another Promise to get the blog's posts. So, we get nested Promises that will be resolved one after the other in sequence.

After all, this code is quite similar to the callback-based code seen in previous examples. However the Promise-based approach give us more flexibility and is more powerful, as we will see shortly.

As a first step, let's rewrite the previous code in a more readable form:

```
function getUserData() {
  return httpGet("/users/12345");
}

function getBlog(user) {
  return httpGet("/blogs/" + user.blogId);
}

function displayBlog(blog) {
  displayPostList(blog.posts);
}

getUserData()
  .then(function(user) {
    getBlog(user)
      .then(function(blog) {
        displayPostList(blog.posts);
      })
  })
```

We used named functions to make the code more readable. However, we can do better.

In fact, the `then()` method always returns a new Promise so that we can chain calls as highlighted in the following code:

```
function getUserData() {
  return httpGet("/users/12345");
}

function getBlog(user) {
  return httpGet("/blogs/" + user.blogId);
}

function displayBlog(blog) {
  displayPostList(blog.posts);
}

getUserData()
  .then(getBlog)
  .then(displayBlog);
```

In our example, the `getUserData()` and `getBlog()` functions return the Promises created by the `httpGet()` function. The `then()` method returns these Promises allowing us to chain the calls. However, more in us, the `then()` method always returns a Promise, even when a Promise handler does not explicitly create and return it.

In fact, when a Promise handler does not return a Promise but a standard value, such as a primitive value or an object, the `then()` method creates a new Promise and resolves it with the returned value. If the Promise handler does not return anything, the `then()` method creates anyway a new resolved Promise and returns it.

Catching failures

In the previous examples, we used the `then()` method of a Promise in order to manage its resolved value. However, a Promise can also be rejected when something goes wrong. It should be pointed out that rejections happen when a Promise is explicitly rejected, but also implicitly if an error is thrown in the constructor callback. We can manage a Promise rejection by passing a second handler function to the `then()` method.

So, our previous code becomes as follows:

```
function getUserData() {
  return httpGet("/users/12345");
}

function getBlog(user) {
```

```
    return httpGet("/blogs/" + user.blogId);
}

function displayBlog(blog) {
    displayPostList(blog.posts);
}

function manageError(error) {
    console.log(error.message);
}

getUserData()
    .then(getBlog, manageError)
    .then(displayBlog, manageError);
```

Here, we introduced the `manageError()` function whose task is simply to show the error message on the console. This function is passed as the second parameter of the `then()` method, and it will be executed when the Promise is rejected.

In this example, we use the same handler for managing Promise rejections, but of course, we can use specific handlers for each Promise. It only depends on how we want to manage rejections.

We have already seen that the second parameter of the `then()` method is optional. Also, the first parameter is optional. In fact, we can pass `null` as the first parameter of `then()` pointing out that we want to manage just Promise rejections. For example, we could write the following code:

```
getUserData()
    .then(null, manageError);
```

This code will ignore the resolved Promise and will only manage possible errors. From a practical point of view, this has little meaning in the specific case. However, we can use this approach to explicitly separate the resolved Promise management from its possible rejection, as in the following:

```
getUserData()
    .then(getBlog)
    .then(null, manageError);
```

Thanks to the call chaining mechanism, the rejected Promise passes from a `then()` invocation to the subsequent one. In fact, when a Promise is rejected and a rejection handler is not specified, a new Promise is internally created with the same rejection reason and it is passed to the subsequent `then()` in order to be managed. This failure propagation allows us to use just one rejection handler function, when we manage all failures in the same way. So, we can rewrite the previous example as follows:

```
getUserData()
  .then(getBlog)
  .then(displayBlog)
  .then(null, manageError);
```

Here, the `manageError()` function will manage any rejection that occurs in any point of the Promise chain.

Instead of using `null` as the first parameter of the `then()` method, we can use an equivalent syntax based on the `catch()` method of the Promise object. So, the preceding code is equivalent to the following:

```
getUserData()
  .then(getBlog)
  .then(displayBlog)
  .catch(manageError);
```

As we can see, the use of the Promises allows to create not only more readable code, but also more robust code, since now we have the ability to intercept and appropriately handle asynchronous errors.

Composing Promises

The example that we used to show how to consume a Promise was a simplified version of the one we used when we introduced the callback approach. In fact, now we have only focused on showing the blog's posts of the user, omitting displaying photos. Let's recall the original code:

```
function getUserBlogAndPhoto(user) {
  getBlog(user.blogId);
  getPhotos(user.albumId);
}

function getBlog(blogId) {
  httpGet("/blogs/" + blogId, displayBlog);
}
```

```
function displayBlog(blog) {
  displayPostList(blog.posts);
}

function getPhotos(albumId) {
  httpGet("/photos/" + user.albumId,  displayAlbum);
}

function displayAlbum(album) {
  displayPhotoList(album.photos);
}

httpGet("/users/12345",  getUserBlogAndPhoto);
```

Applying what we learned about Promises, we can rewrite it as in the following example:

```
function getUserData() {
  return httpGet("/users/12345");
}

function getBlog(user) {
  return httpGet("/blogs/" + user.blogId);
}

function displayBlog(blog) {
  displayPostList(blog.posts);
}

function getPhotos(user) {
  return httpGet("/photos/" + user.albumId);
}

function displayAlbum(album) {
  displayPhotoList(album.photos);
}

function manageError(error) {
  console.log(error.message);
}

function getBlogAndPhotos(user) {
  getBlog(user)
    .then(displayBlog);

  getPhotos(user)
    .then(displayAlbum);
}
```

```
getUserData()
  .then(getBlogAndPhotos)
  .catch(manageError);
```

All we have done here is to integrate the previous Promise-based code with a new HTTP call to retrieve the photos associated with the user. We introduced the `getBlogAndPhotos()` function to handle the two asynchronous tasks that will retrieve both posts and photos. But, how Promises will be handled in this case? What happens if one Promise is resolved and the other one is rejected?

If both Promises created inside the `getBlogAndPhotos()` function are resolved, we will get posts and photos displayed on the page. The order in which they will be displayed is not determined-they will be displayed as they will be received and the Promise is resolved.

However, unlike what we would expect, if one or both Promises are rejected, we will not get them managed as we planned. The `manageError()` function will not be called. In fact, accordingly to what we said about the chaining mechanism of the `then()` method, if our resolved Promise handler does not return anything, as in our case, a new resolved Promise is created and passed to the subsequent handler in the chain. So, when the `getBlogAndPhotos()` function is executed, it implicitly passes a resolved Promise to the next handler. Since we have a `catch()` method, the resolved Promise is ignored and the chain of Promises is considered as resolved. When one or both Promises created by the `getBlog()` and `getPhotos()` functions are rejected, they will no longer be able to pass to the `catch()` method, since it is no longer waiting for their settling.

When we need to get the result of a multiple asynchronous task, we should use the `all()` method of the Promise constructor. This method allows us to wait for all associated Promises be resolved. So, we can synchronize the asynchronous tasks and manage their results all at once. The `Promise.all()` method takes an array of Promises and creates a Promise that will be resolved when all of them are resolved. When all the Promises in the array are resolved, an array with the correspondent resolved values will be passed to the handler function. If any of the Promises is rejected, the entire array of Promises are rejected and the `catch()` method is called.

So, we can use the `Promise.all()` method in order to wait for a blog's posts and photos availability before displaying their content. This allows us to decide the content's display order and to correctly manage possible rejection. Now, we can rewrite our code as in the following:

```
getUserData()
  .then(function(user) {
    var promises = [];
    var blog = getBlog(user);
```

```
      var album = getAlbum(user);

      promises.push(blog);
      promises.push(photos);

      Promise.all(promises)
      .then(function(results) {
        displayBlog(results[0]);
       displayAlbum(results[1]);
      })
   })
   .catch(manageError);
```

We defined a `promises` array and filled it with the Promises created by calling the `getBlog()` and `getAlbum()` functions. This array is then passed to the `Promise.all()` method, which creates the new Promise we will consume. When both Promises are resolved, we will display the data returned by the server in the order we prefer. In the example, we first display the blog's posts and then the photos. If any rejection occurs, the `catch()` method will be executed as expected.

An alternative way to manage multiple asynchronous tasks is by the `Promise.race()` method. Like the `Promise.all()` method, `race()` takes an array of Promises and creates a new Promise as well. However, it resolves the new created Promise when any of the Promises contained in the array is resolved.

We can use this feature to display the first content that becomes available after submitting the requests of posts and photos to the server. The following code shows how to implement it:

```
   Promise.race(promises)
     .then(function(result) {
       if (result.posts) displayBlog(results);
       if (result.photos) displayAlbum(results);
     })
     .catch(manageError);
```

The Promise associated with the `promises` array is resolved when the blog's posts or the photos are received. So, in the handler we check which content has been received and call the respective function to display it.

Using Generators

The Promise-based approach to manage asynchronous tasks gives us a powerful tool to write a more readable code and have better control over their execution. However, the style we use to write code still needs to be conscious of the asynchronous nature of the tasks. Even if we can do without nesting callbacks using the `then()` and `catch()` methods and composing Promises using the `all()` and `race()` methods, we are essentially calling callbacks anyway. An ideal approach should let us write asynchronous code in the same way we write synchronous code. We can make something similar using the new ECMAScript 6 Generators.

Introducing Generators

The ES6 **Generators** are functions that can be paused. Unlike normal functions that runs until they reach the end or execute a `return` statement, a Generator can be suspended and then can be resumed. Let's take a look at a simple Generator like the following:

```
function *counter() {
  yield 1;
  yield 2;
  yield 3;
}
```

From a syntactic point of view, the first thing we notice is the star by the function name. This simply states that it is a Generator. The other new thing is the `yield` keyword. This keyword is a statement that pauses the execution of the Generator, that is, when the `yield` statement is reached, the execution of the function is suspended at that point.

Unlike a normal function, when we call a Generator, we get an object that represents the Generator itself. This object has a `next()` method that allows us to start the execution of the Generator or resume it when it has been paused. For example, we can start our `counter()` generator with the following code:

```
var myCounter = counter();

myCounter.next();
```

The `next()` method makes the body of the Generator run until a `yield` statement is reached. In our example, the first `yield` statement is executed, and as a result of its execution, an object is returned. The returned object has two properties: the `value` property containing the value of the expression to the right of the `yield` statement and the `done` property whose Boolean value says if the execution of the Generator has terminated (*true*) or it is simply suspended (*false*). Let's consider the following code to understand which values will be returned by our Generator:

```
var myCounter = counter();

myCounter.next();   //{value: 1, done: false}
myCounter.next();   //{value: 2, done: false}
myCounter.next();   //{value: 3, done: false}
myCounter.next();   //{value: undefined, done: true}
```

As we can see, each time we call the `next()` method, the execution of the body of the Generator resumes from the point it was suspended until it reaches the end of the function.

Using Generators for asynchronous tasks

After briefly seeing what Generators are, we may ask ourselves what they have to do with asynchronous code. The ability to suspend and resume the execution of standard JavaScript code can help us give the synchronous form to asynchronous tasks. Let's explain with an example. Consider the `httpGet()` function we introduced when talking about callbacks:

```
function httpGet(url, callback) {
  var httpReq = new XMLHttpRequest();

  httpReq.onreadystatechange = function() {
    var data;

    if (httpReq.readyState == 4 && httpReq.status == 200) {
      data = JSON.parse(httpReq.responseText);
      callback(data);
    } else {
      throw new Error(httpReq.statusText);
    }
  };

  httpReq.open("GET", url, true);
  httpReq.send();
}
```

We can use it in order to define a `request()` function as in the following:

```
function request(url) {
  httpGet(url, function(response) {
    myDataGenerator.next(response);
  });
}
```

The `request()` function may seem a little cryptic. Actually, it calls the `httpGet()` function to make the asynchronous call, and when a result comes from the server, it resumes a Generator called `myDataGenerator`. Let's see what this Generator looks like:

```
function *dataGenerator() {
  var user = yield request("/users/12345");
  var blog = yield request("/blogs/" + user.blogId);

  displayPostList(blog.posts);
}
```

The `dataGenerator()` function is the heart of our control over the asynchronous tasks. While keeping a synchronous programming style, we can coordinate the asynchronous Ajax calls in a very simple way. However, the initial step that makes all working is missing:

```
var myDataGenerator = dataGenerator();

myDataGenerator.next();
```

We get the Generator and start its execution by invoking the `next()` method.

Starting the Generator, we submit the request of the user's data to the server and pause its execution. When the server returns the requested data, the callback resumes the Generator's execution by calling the `next()` method and passing the response. This response is assigned to the `user` variable inside the Generator and then a new request of the user's blog is submitted and again the Generator pauses. Once the blog data is received, the Generator resumes again, assigns the new response to the `blog` variable, and finally displays its posts by calling the `displayPostList()` function.

The final result is an asynchronous code written as if it was synchronous. This example, however, is very rudimentary since it does not consider failures. We could combine the Generator approach with the Promise approach in order to get the best of both.

ES7 async/await

The model of code writing using Generators is similar to the pattern proposed by the `async` functions in the future ECMAScript 7 specifications. Basically, it follows the style described in our example without using the Generator infrastructure. So, in the near future, we will write the following code to get the same result:

```
async function displayUserPosts() {
  var user = await httpGet("/users/12345");
  var blog = await httpGet("/blogs/" + user.blogId);

  displayPostList(blog.posts);
}

displayUserPosts();
```

Notice the use of the `async` keyword that marks the `displayUserPosts()` function as asynchronous and the `await` keyword that allows us to suspend the function execution waiting to get a result.

Summary

This chapter discussed how we can face asynchronous programming in JavaScript. Starting with the asynchronous nature of the JavaScript's runtime execution flow, we explored how to manage events using callback functions. We saw that, although callbacks are widely used to manage asynchronous code, they are not so effective. A heavy use of callbacks leads to unreadable code and the so-called callback hellâ⊚⊚a maze of code difficult to read and understand. Moreover, managing asynchronous code with callbacks do not allows us to catch failures.

Promises can help us get more control on asynchronous code. We have seen the standard Promise's API of ECMAScript 6 and shown how to use them in order to catch results and failure and synchronize multiple asynchronous tasks.

Then, we approached the asynchronous code management using a technique based on Generators, a new feature of ECMAScript 6 as well. This approach allows us to manage asynchronous code by writing code in a synchronous style. This technique appears to be a forerunner of the `async` functions in discussion for ECMAScript 7 specifications.

In the following chapter, we will take a look at how to organize our code in order to make it modular and reusable.

10
Organizing Code

We rarely worry about code organization for simple scripts, since a few lines of code may be immediately identified and possibly changed without any issues. But when the codebase of our application grows, the need to organize our code becomes increasingly urgent. In this chapter, we will describe the most common ways to face this problem starting from namespaces through the ECMAScript 6 modules. In the middle, we will explore the different approaches to define organizational units of the code that fit on the server-side and on client-side the JavaScript programming.

The following topics will be discussed in the chapter:

- The global scope
- The namespace pattern
- The module pattern
- Approaches to JavaScript modularization (AMD and CommonJS)
- ES6 modules

The global scope

When JavaScript was born, its role was very limited. It was mainly used for event handling and for some visual effects, acting as the glue between the user and the HTML document. Usually, this purpose did not require too much code and most of its organization relied on functions and files. The global scope was the natural living environment of publicly accessible variables and functions.

With the growth of JavaScript's capability, the evolution of object models and the spread of the language also in a context different from the browser, the importance of JavaScript's role has grown as well, and so has the code size. What once was a simple set of scripts, now has become an application. The global scope is no longer a suitable environment to put code without criteria.

The use of global scope has always been an anti-pattern in any programming language for various reasons:

- **Understandability issues**: When the code size of an application is not trivial, reasoning about a snippet of code that makes reference to a global variable may be difficult, since its value may be changed by any other part of the application and we cannot have control over it.
- **Implicit coupling**: References to global variables, objects, or functions create an implicit coupling making code reuse impossible.
- **Namespace pollution**: The global scope is an open environmentâøøevery snippet of code may access it and add new items without control; this may lead to a confused heap of variables, objects, functions difficult to read and with a high risk of naming clash.
- **Memory allocation issues**: Global items are alive throughout the application life, and their memory footprint may be significant even if they are not used.

In a dynamic language such as JavaScript, these issues are even more amplified. Let's see some side effects we can have by relying on the global scope.

Global definitions

As we know, JavaScript is very permissive. If we do not declare a variable, it is created on our behalf. Of course, this is a bad practice that always should be avoided by enabling *strict mode* using the `"use strict"`; clause. In fact, if we rely on this behavior to create global variables, we have no control over their existence nor on their management. We define a global variable in the following example:

```
function myFunction() {
  globalVar = "This is a global variable";

  return globalVar;
}
```

The assignment to the `globalVar` variable implicitly creates it in the global scope. So, in another part of the application, we have another code snippet that creates another variable with the same name. We are assigning a new value to the existing variable as follows:

```
function anotherFunction() {
  globalVar = { name: "John", surname: "Smith"};

  return globalVar;
}
```

Since we have no control over global scope, we cannot avoid naming clashes of variables and consequently undesired assignments. This is particularly true when we want to reuse a piece of code in another application. Moreover, when we read the code, not always it is obvious which value has a global variable in a given file, and this may lead to misunderstandings.

Of course, the same problem happens with functions defined in the global scope. In fact, if we define a new function with the same name of an existing one, the last definition overrides the previous one. So, when the amount of code of an application grows without any organization, we might risk redefining existing functions with obvious bad effects. Think of the creation of a library; how can we make sure that our functions or our variables do not collide with the functions and variables existing in the application that will use it?

Creating namespaces

In order to reduce the negative impact of using the global scope, we should avoid creating global objects unless they are absolutely necessary. A first approach to avoid the global scope pollution and organizing our code is to use namespaces. A **namespace** is a collection of names used to identify objects in a given context. The purpose of namespaces is to avoid confusion and collisions with objects having the same names in another context, providing a way to group names together by category.

Many programming languages support namespaces in order to organize blocks of functionality in our application into easily manageable groups that can be uniquely identified. JavaScript has no built-in support for namespaces, but we can use objects and closures in order to create similar structures.

Namespaces as object literals

A first and simple way to emulate a namespace in JavaScript is using like object literal like the one shown here:

```
var myApplication = {
  version: "1.0",
  name: "My Application",
  config: {...},
  init: function() {...}
};
```

In this example, we can see a variable declaration which is assigned to an object literal describing an application. The use of object literals as namespaces has the advantage of reducing the pollution of the global scope and helps to organize code and variables logically. We can access such namespaces as in the following example:

```
console.log(myApplication.name);    //My Application
myApplication.init();
```

It's possible to span a single namespace across multiple files. If data is well structured, this can help the reader to easily navigate the code. In this case, it is important to check if the variable to which the namespace is assigned already exists before defining it, as in the following example:

```
var myApplication = myApplication || {};
myApplication = {
  version: "1.0",
  name: "My Application",
  config: {...},
  init: function() {...}
};
```

Namespaces can have a hierarchical structure. We can define nested namespaces very easily as follows:

```
var myApplication = {
  version: "1.0",
  name: "My Application",
  config: {
    ui: {
      backgroundColor: "green",
      fontSize: 12
    },
    localization: {
      language: "english",
      dateFormat: "MM-dd-yyyy"
```

```
    }
  },
  init: function() {...}
};
```

Or, for better readability, we can define it by making many explicit assignments:

```
var myApplication = {
  version: "1.0",
  name: "My Application",
  init: function() {...}
};

myApplication.config: {};
myApplication.config.ui: {
  backgroundColor: "green",
  fontSize: 12
};
myApplication.config.localization: {
  language: "english",
  dateFormat: "MM-dd-yyyy"
};
```

As we expect, we can access nested namespaces as nested objects, which they actually are:

```
myApplication.config.localization.language: "italian",
myApplication.config.localization.dateFormat = "dd-MM-yyyy";
```

In order to get a better performance when multiple accesses are made to a sub-namespace, we should use an alias, as shown in the following:

```
var localizationConfig = myApplication.config.localization;
localizationConfig.language: "italian",
localizationConfig.dateFormat = "dd-MM-yyyy";
```

The benefit of using object literals as namespaces is that they offer us a very simple and elegant key/value syntax to work with.

Defining namespaces with IIFE

Using object literals as namespaces is extremely simple and convenient, but this approach still uses a global variable, even if it is well identified. If having one known variable as namespace may be acceptable in an application under our control, it should be avoided in libraries or components that should be used inside a context out of our control. In this case, we should leave to the programmer the decision concerning the name of the global variable. A possible solution is based on the use of an **Immediately Invoked Function Expression** or **IIFE**, as in the following example:

```
var myApplication = {};

(function(nameSpace) {
  nameSpace.version = "1.0",
  nameSpace.name = "My Application",
  nameSpace.config = {/*...*/},
  nameSpace.init = function() {/*...*/}
})(myApplication);
```

Here, we define the variable `myApplication` that is assigned an empty object literal and pass it to an IIFE that attaches the content of the namespace. The user of our namespace definition can decide the name of the global variable avoiding name clashes. For example, instead of using the `myApplication` variable, they might decide to declare a variable with a different name. They might also decide to assign the namespace to a local variable instead of using a global one.

A variant of the previous approach uses the `this` keyword instead to rely on the `nameSpace` parameter:

```
var myApplication = {};

(function() {
  this.version: "1.0",
  this.name: "My Application",
  this.config: {...},
  this.init: function() {...}
}).apply(myApplication);
```

An interesting aspect of using an IIFE to define a namespace is that we can define and use private variables inside the body of the IIFE:

```
var myApplication = {};

(function(nameSpace) {
  var i = 0;
```

```
    nameSpace.version = "1.0",
    nameSpace.name = "My Application",
    nameSpace.counter = function() { return i++;};
})(myApplication);
```

This can be useful when we need an internal state that cannot be accessed by external code.

The module pattern

A module is a standalone software component implementing specific functionalities, and is easily reusable in different applications. It enables modular programming whose goal is to simplify the development, testing, and maintenance of large applications possibly involving many developers. Modules can also be packaged and deployed separately from each other, allowing changes on a particular module to be properly isolated from the rest of the code of an application. Splitting an application in multiple modules has many benefits: in addition to code reusability, it forces us to reason about the architecture of an application and to structure it so that it may result in becoming more understandable for people who aren't familiar with our application's code.

Modules versus namespaces

In the previous section, we introduced namespaces as an approach to organize our code in nested areas. Now, we are talking about modules as another way to organize the code of an application. What are the differences between these two ways of organizing code?

Namespaces are hierarchical containers for variables and functions. Their main goal is to organize names in order to avoid conflicts and redefinitions.

Modules avoid name conflicts and redefinitions as well, but they are mainly focused on functionalities; in fact, they provide mechanisms to export functionalities, to allow reuse of code, and to manage dependencies on other modules.

In the rest of the chapter, we will see different approaches to implement modules in JavaScript.

Using anonymous closures

The classic pattern to implement a module in JavaScript relies on the nature of an IIFE and is usually known as the **module pattern**. Since the closure of a function allows us to create a private context, we can implement functionalities inside the body of an IIFE and export only what we want to make publicly available. The following example defines a module that exports two geometry functions:

```
var geoModule = (function() {
  var pi = 3.14;

  function circumference(radius) {
    return 2*pi*radius;
  }

  function circleArea(radius) {
    return pi*radius*radius;
  }

  return {
    calculateCircumference:  circumference,
    calculateCircleArea:    circleArea
  };
})();
```

We can see that the anonymous function is immediately executed and its result is assigned to a variable. The body of the function defines the `circumference()` and `circleArea()` functions and returns an object with two methods mapped to these functions. We say that the module **exports** the members of the returned object. Note that the exported members may have different names from the one defined internally. Thanks to the closure, the code that will use this module will not have access to the private functions and variables, but will be able to use just the exported members.

We can use the members exported by the previous code using the object assigned to the `geoModule` variable, as shown in the following example:

```
console.log(geoModule.calculateCircumference (5));
//result: 31.400000000000002

console.log(geoModule.calculateCircleArea(5));
//result: 78.5
```

Of course a module can export not only a standard function, but also constructor functions, literal objects, or any other item. The following example shows a module that exports a constructor function:

```
var myModule = (function() {
  function Person(name, surname) {
    this.name = name;
    this.surname = surname;
  }

  return {
    Person:  Person
  };
})();

var johnSmith = new myModule.Person("John", "Smith");
```

Importing modules

A module can use the exported member of another module in order to implement its own functionalities. In this case, we say that the module **imports** another module. This also means that the current module **depends** on the other module.

We can import existing modules in our module by passing them as a parameter of the IIFE. The following example shows the previous module that imports the standard `Math` module:

```
var geoModule = (function(mathModule) {
  var pi = mathModule.PI;

  function circumference(radius) {
    return 2*pi*radius;
  }

  function circleArea(radius) {
    return pi*mathModule.pow(radius, 2);
  }

  return {
    calculateCircumference:  circumference,
    calculateCircleArea:     circleArea
  };
})(Math);
```

As we can see, the `Math` module is passed as a parameter of the IIFE and it is used inside its body. We will continue to call the module's members as before:

```
console.log(geoModule.calculateCircumference(5));
//result: 31.41592653589793

console.log(geoModule.calculateCircleArea(5));
//result: 78.53981633974483
```

Although the `Math` object is globally available, it is a good practice to pass a module explicitly. This helps in understanding the existing dependencies between different modules and help us to possibly replace the module on which it depends with another one with the same interface. In other words, by explicitly importing a dependency we are able to decouple modules. Moreover, using a local variable or parameter to reference a global object is often a good idea because it shortens the lookup chain and could possibly improve performance.

Augmenting modules

Usually, a module is contained in a single file. In general, it is a good practice since it allows us to easily identify the functionality implemented by an application. In some situations, however, we may need to extend the functionalities implemented in a module without modifying the module itself. For example, suppose we have a module that implements standard geometry functions. In a specific function, we need to add some new geometry functions that logically should belong to the geometry module, but they are specific for the current application and we do not want to add them directly to the geometry module's file. The idea is to create a new file that implements the new functions augmenting the existing geometry module. We can achieve this goal by augmenting the geometry module as shown by the following example:

```
geoModule = (function(mathModule, me) {
  me.calculateSphereVolume = function(radius) {
    return 4*mathModule.PI*mathModule.pow(radius, 2);
  };

  return me;
})(Math, geoModule);
```

In this example, we pass the geometry module `geoModule` as a parameter to the IIFE that defines the new module. The body of the function adds the `calculateSphereVolume()` method to the original module and returns it. We get exactly what we wantedâ⊚⊚a new module that adds functions to an existing module without altering the original module definition.

We can call the new `calculateSphereVolume()` method as it were defined in the original module definition:

```
console.log(geoModule.calculateCircumference (5));
//result: 31.41592653589793

console.log(geoModule.calculateCircleArea(5));
//result: 78.53981633974483

console.log(geoModule.calculateSphereVolume(5));
//result: 314.1592653589793
```

If we identify the existing module as our application, this approach allows us to cleanly import a module without introducing any new global variables: the module augments the current application's environment.

Loose augmentation

The example of module augmentation we have seen earlier requires that our original module must be created before the module that augments it. We can drop this constraint and make sure that two or more modules can augment each other regardless of their loading order. This is usually called **loose augmentation**. Let's take a look at the following code:

```
geoModule = (function(mathModule, me) {
  me.calculateSphereVolume = function(radius) {
    return 4*mathModule.PI*mathModule.pow(radius, 2);
  };

  return me;
})(Math, geoModule || {});
```

It is almost identical to the previous example. The only difference is the expression `geoModule || {}` that initializes the `geoModule` variable with an empty object if it is undefined, that is, the module has still not been created.

Overriding a module's methods

In addition to augmenting a module, we may need to override an existing method. We can easily do it as follows:

```
geoModule = (function(me) {
  var oldCalculateCircleArea = me.calculateCircleArea;
```

```
  me.calculateCircleArea = function(radius) {
    return oldCalculateCircleArea(radius).toFixed(2);
  };

  return me;
})(geoModule);
```

Here, we define a version of the `calculateCircleArea()` function that always has two decimal positions. As we can see, we assigned the new definition to the `calculateCircleArea` member of the module. Notice how we made a copy of the original method, since it is needed inside the new definition.

Now, we can call the new definition of the `calculateCircleArea()` function like before, even if we get a different result:

```
console.log(geoModule.calculateCircleArea(5));
//result: 78.54
```

Tight augmentation

The loose augmentation is a very nice way to extend modules. However, not always can it be safely used. For example, we cannot use module members or override them if we are not sure that the original module has been loaded. In these cases, we need to use **tight augmentation**, which requires modules to be loaded in a specified order. In this way, we are sure that a module member is available before using it.

Here is a simple example of a module that needs tight augmentation:

```
geoModule = (function(me) {

  me.calculateCircleBiArea = function(radius) {
    return me.calculateCircleArea(radius)*2;
  };

  return me;
})(geoModule);
```

In the example, the `calculateCircleBiArea()` function relies on the `calculateCircleArea()` function, so the module that defines `calculateCircleArea()` must be loaded before the current one. We can call these methods as follows:

```
console.log(geoModule.calculateCircleArea(5));
//result: 78.53981633974483
```

```
console.log(geoModule.calculateCircleBiArea(5));
//result: 157.07963267948966
```

Composing modules

We can combine two or more modules together in order to create a new module that contains all their functionalities. This can be easily achieved by augmenting one module with the members of the other one, as shown here:

```
var geoModule = (function(module1, module2) {
  var me =  module1;

  for (var memberName in module2) {
    if (module2.hasOwnProperty(memberName)) {
      me[memberName] = module2[memberName];
    }
  }

  return me;
})(circleModule, polygonModule);
```

In this example, we create a geometry module by combining a module specialized in circle management and a module that can handle polygons. If a name clash occurs, the member in the second module overwrites the member of the first one. Of course, we can change the name clash strategy by changing the way we assign members to the new module.

ECMAScript 6 introduced the `Object.assign()` method so that we can combine modules by simply writing:

```
var geoModule = (function(module1, module2) {

  return Object.assign(module1, module2);

})(circleModule, polygonModule);
```

Submodules

As for namespaces, we can create nested modules or **submodules** by simply attaching a new module to a property of the main module. In the following example, we attached to geoModule a new module called `triangleModule`:

```
geoModule.triangleModule = (function() {

  function perimeter(side1, side2, side3) {
```

```
      return side1+side2+side3;
   }

   function area(basis, height) {
     return basis*height/2;
   }

   return {
      calculateTrianglePerimeter:  perimeter,
      calculateTriangleArea:    area
   };

})();
```

We can use the submodule as shown below:

```
geoModule.triangleModule.calculateTriangleArea(3,4);    //result:  6
```

Module loading

Modules concern code organization, which is how the functionalities of an application are distributed in units that simplify reusability, maintainability, and understandability of the code. The concept of module itself does not concern how it is loaded into the execution environment. Usually, this should be a concern of the runtime engine hosting the application. However, module loading plays an important role in JavaScript, as we will see in this section.

Modules, scripts, and files

In the examples we have shown so far, we have not said where the modules are. Until now, we talked about modules as units of code with private and public parts, but where do they live in an application?

In general, one or more modules can be in the same container of the entire application. For example, we can imagine a JavaScript application composed of many modules, all stored in a single file or in a single Web page. For nontrivial applications usually this is not a clever solution, at least during the development stage. Having all the code in a single file does not simplify its understandability nor its reusability. A better approach is to store one module into one file so that it becomes easier to detect which module implements a certain functionality and to reuse a module in another application.

In a runtime environment, being able to access a filesystem, such as in server-side environments like Node.js, loading modules from files is not a problem. It can be a synchronous or asynchronous operation usually with a minor impact on the overall performance.

Conversely, loading a module in a web page may cause issues. Usually, we place JavaScript code inside a `<script>` element, as in the following example:

```
<script type="text/javascript">
  (function(module) {
    module.calculateTriangleArea = function area(basis, height) {
      return basis*height/2;
    };

    return module;
  })(myApp);
</script>
```

Or, even better, its code can be placed in an external file, as shown below:

```
<script type="text/javascript" src="triangleModule.js"></script>
```

In both cases, the code will make the module available to the application. However, while in the first case the code of the module is loaded within the entire page, in the second case the code needs to be loaded after a new request to the server. In the latter case, the browser loads the file containing the code and executes it, blocking in the meanwhile the rendering of the page. Since loading scripts may be slower on the Internet and a browser opens a limited number of concurrent HTTP connections, this approach may heavily affect the user experience.

In order to avoid this issue, we need to load scripts in the background with no impact on page renderingâ◎◎we need asynchronous loading. HTML provides us with a couple of attributes of the `<script>` tag: `defer` and `async`.

We can use `defer` as shown here:

```
<script type="text/javascript" src="triangleModule.js" defer>
</script>
```

This ensures that the script is loaded during the page parsing and is executed after the parsing has completed. The execution order of the scripts reflects their appearance order in the document. These attributes may be useful when we want to be sure that our code runs when the document has been parsed, but anyway its loading slows down the page rendering.

We can use the `async` attribute as in the following example:

```
<script type="text/javascript" src="triangleModule.js" async>
</script>
```

It allows us to load scripts asynchronously without any immediate impact on the page rendering. The script's code is executed as soon as it is loaded, but we have no guarantee on the execution order of scripts.

A simple module loader

When the codebase of an application becomes large, we may feel that the built-in loading mechanism of the runtime environment is no longer adequate. We may need to load modules conditionally, resolve dependencies between modules or make some other processing while getting a module. In these cases, we may need a module loader.

There is a clear distinction between **script loader** and **module loader**. A **script loader** is a mechanism that loads a piece of code and executes it without caring about its structure. A **module loader** is a mechanism that loads a module, it is a piece of code that has a certain structure and the loader knows how to interact with it.

We can write a module loader in a very simple way. Let's implement a `loadModule()` function that takes a module name, loads that module's file from the filesystem or the Web, depending on the platform we are running on, and returns the exported functionalities. We supposed to have a `getFileContent()` function, which returns the content of a given file as a string. The code of our simple module loader may be as follows:

```
function loadModule(moduleName) {
    var moduleCode = new Function("return " + getFileContent    (moduleName));

    return moduleCode();
}
```

In the example, we exploited the `Function()` constructor that allows us to create a new function object from a string representing its body. We can optionally define one or more parameters, but in our example it is not necessary. The new function is then executed and its output is returned to the caller. Our module loader relies on the fact that the module is defined using the standard module pattern that returns an object with the exported methods.

So, we can use our loader as follows:

```
var geoModule = loadModule("geoModule.js");

geoModule.calculateCircleArea(5);
```

Someone may ask why we used the `Function()` constructor and not the `eval()` function. Using the `eval()` function is not usually a good idea. In fact, evaluating a JavaScript piece of code may cause an unclear mix of local and global scope. Consider, for example, the following code:

```
var declaration = "var x = 123;";

function evaluate(code) {
  eval(code);
  return x;
}

console.log(evaluate(declaration));   //result: 123
console.log(x);                       //result: undefined
```

It defines a string variable with a declaration of a variable x. The string is evaluated inside the `evaluate()` function. This creates a local variable, as we can deduce from the output. This is not the case if we use `window.eval()`, as we can see in the following example:

```
var declaration = "var x = 123;";

function evaluate(code) {
  window.eval(code);
  return x;
}

console.log(evaluate(declaration));   //result: 123
console.log(x);                       //result: 123
```

Of course, our simple module loader implementation has several issues. For example, if many modules depend on the same module, the `loadModule()` function will be called multiple times always loading the same module. This issue can be solved by storing the modules that have already been loaded in an object that acts as a cache. When a module is requested, it will be searched inside the cache before loading it from the server. Let's take a look at how our code changes:

```
function loadModule(moduleName) {
  var moduleCode;
  var module;

  if (moduleName in loadModule.cache) {
```

```
        module =  loadModule.cache[moduleName];
    } else {
        moduleCode = new Function("return " + getFileContent
        (moduleName));
        module = moduleCode();
        loadModule.cache[moduleName] = module;
    }

    return module;
}

loadModule.cache = {};
```

The caching issue is just one of the problems that a module loader has to face. Other features required for a module loader concern synchronous or asynchronous loading, dependency management, recursive loading, and so on. So, but not always, writing our own module loader is the best choice. Nowadays, several module loaders exist, and we can choose the best one that fits our needs. A first choice we have to make when selecting a module loader is the paradigm it implements. Currently, we have two module loading paradigms: **CommonJS module** and **Asynchronous Module Definition**.

CommonJS modules

The CommonJS community attempts to define standards for JavaScript in order to make JavaScript engine implementations more compatible. We mentioned them in Chapter 9, *Asynchronous Programming and Promises*, when discussing about Promises. **CommonJS modules** specify an API that modules use to declare dependencies. The file containing the JavaScript code is the module, so there is no need for a function wrapper to contain the scope as happens in the module pattern, because each file is given its own scope. Modules declare dependencies with a synchronous require() function. That means that execution is blocked while the required module is being resolved. This allows us to use the module immediately after requiring it.

Before Node.js, there were several other attempts to run JavaScript on the server side. Both Netscape and Microsoft supported JavaScript in their server environments in the 90s and more recently Rhino gained some popularity. Each JavaScript server-side environment used different conventions for dealing with module loading. CommonJS was created to solve that problems and Node-style modules are essentially an implementation of the CommonJS module specification.

A module must explicitly export an object with the functionalities to make it publicly available. This can be made with the `exports` property of the `module` object. Let's see how we can write a CommonJS module:

```
var pi = 3.14;

function circumference(radius) {
  return 2*pi*radius;
}

function circleArea(radius) {
  return pi*radius*radius;
}

module.exports = {
  calculateCircumference:   circumference,
  calculateCircleArea:    circleArea
};
```

If we put the preceding code in a file named `geoModule.js`, we can load the module as follows:

```
var geoModule = require("./geoModule");

console.log(geoModule.calculateCircumference(5));
```

As we can see, the CommonJS approach to manage modules is extremely simple and guarantees the order of execution of modules. However, it is not suitable for browsers since module loading is synchronous and it blocks the page rendering.

Asynchronous Module Definition

An alternative approach to CommonJS specifically designed for browsers is the **Asynchronous Module Definition** paradigm or **AMD**. As the name says, its main feature is asynchronous loading of modules. In order to create an AMD module, we need to use the `define()` function that takes three parameters:

- A string that represents the name of the module
- An array of dependencies expressed as module names or file locations
- A function containing the module's code

Anything returned by the module is exposed to the outside world. Let's rewrite our module following the AMD standard:

```
define("geoModule", [], function() {
  var pi = 3.14;

  function circumference(radius) {
    return 2*pi*radius;
  }

  function circleArea(radius) {
    return pi*radius*radius;
  }

  return {
    calculateCircumference:  circumference,
    calculateCircleArea:     circleArea
  };

});
```

We assigned the `geoModule` name to the module using the `define()` function. Then, we passed an empty array to declare that our module has no dependencies and finally passed the function that contains the module's code.

Now, we can load our module as shown in the following example:

```
require(["geoModule"], function(geoModule) {
  console.log(geoModule.calculateCircumference(5));
});
```

We used the `require()` function by passing an array with the name of the module we want to load and a callback function that uses our module. The module's content is mapped to the callback's parameter once it is loaded.

When defining a module, we can omit the first parameter that defines an identifier for the module. In this case, we can identify a module by specifying the filename that contains it. Moreover, we can also omit the dependencies array when it is empty.

Having to do with asynchronous calls, the `require()` function may potentially suffer the same issues we analyzed in Chapter 9, *Asynchronous Programming and Promises*, where we talked about asynchronous programming. Just to recall some of the issues discussed at that time, we cannot catch errors and lose a bit of readability. A better approach could use Promises; but unfortunately, the AMD specification does not support them.

At the time of this writing, RequireJS, the most known AMD implementation, does not support Promises. However, some extensions and plugins like the following allow to use them:

- https://github.com/jokeyrhyme/requirejs-promise
- https://github.com/requirejs/alameda

We can integrate AMD the `require()` function with ES6 Promises as shown in the following example:

```
function requireWithPromise(modules) {
  return new Promise(function(resolve, reject) {
    try {
      require(modules, resolve);
    }
    catch(e) {
      reject(new Error(e.message));
    }
  });
}

requireWithPromise(["geoModule"])
  .then(function(geoModule) {
    console.log(geoModule.calculateCircumference(5));
  })
  .catch(function(error) { console.log(error.message); });
```

The `requireWithPromise()` function takes an array of module names as a parameter and returns a Promise. In this way, we can use the standard methods to manage the Promise, such as `then()` or `catch()`, as in the example, or `all()` and `race()` when we need to synchronize multiple Promises.

The AMD approach to module loading naturally works on browsers. It can load multiple modules concurrently and is very convenient when we do not need to load a module at page load. However, the asynchronous loading is subject to potential race conditions if not properly designed. A common criticism of AMD concerns its syntax, which tends to become hard to understand, especially when the dependencies array grows. Although AMD cannot guarantee the order of execution of asynchronous modules, we can mitigate this issue by combining it with Promises.

Merging the module pattern with AMD

Each module loading paradigm has its own way to define a module, and both differ from the classic module pattern definition. This raises a problem since the way we define a module determines the way it will be loaded. In fact, if we define a module using `define()`, it can only be used with an AMD loader, such as RequireJS or Curl.js. However, we can make modules written using the classic module pattern compatible with AMD. What we need to do is to add a couple of statements at the end of the IIFE body, as shown by the following example:

```
(function() {
  var pi = 3.14;
  var export;

  function circumference(radius) {
    return 2*pi*radius;
  }

  function circleArea(radius) {
    return pi*radius*radius;
  }

  export = {
    calculateCircumference:  circumference,
    calculateCircleArea:     circleArea
  };

  if (typeof define === 'function') {
    define([], function () {
      return export;     }); }


})();
```

The highlighted code checks if a `define()` function is defined. If it is so, an AMD module is defined returning the functionalities assigned to the `export` variable.

In this way, our module can be asynchronously loaded by AMD loaders and still properly works if it's loaded within a simple `<script>` element.

Universal Module Definition

As discussed in the previous section, each module loading approach has its own syntax to define a module. We saw how to make AMD and the module pattern compatible, but what about CommonJS module and AMD compatibility?

UMD

An attempt to define JavaScript modules that are compatible both for AMD and CommonJS paradigms is **Universal Module Definition** or simply **UMD**. It is actually a collection of patterns published on GitHub at the address: `https://github.com/umdjs/umd`. Although there are a lot of different patterns, they are all essentially variations on the same ideaâ⊚⊚to define a module that can be used in CommonJS and AMD environments. The following is a code template of UMD module definition following the pattern called **returnExport**:

```
(function (root, factory) {
  if (typeof define === 'function' && define.amd) {
    // AMD. Register as an anonymous module.
    define([], factory);
  } else if (typeof exports === 'object') {
    // Node. Does not work with strict CommonJS, but
    // only CommonJS-like environments that support
    //module.exports, like Node.
    module.exports = factory();
  } else {
    // Browser globals (root is window)
    root.returnExports = factory();
  }
}(this, function () {
  //Module code
  return {...};
}));
```

Basically, it is an IIFE that takes two parameters: the object to which the module will be attached in a browser context (`root`) and the function that actually defines the module (`factory`). In our example, we pass the `this` keyword as the root, so the module will be attached to the global scope when it is loaded inside a browser without AMD.

This definition makes the module available as a CommonJS module, an AMD module, or a global variable, depending on the environment.

The detection of the environment is made by checking if the key functions of each paradigm exist. In fact, if a `define()` function is detected, then the function builds an AMD module; if an `exports` object exists, then it builds a CommonJS module; otherwise it attaches the module at the global variable `returnExports`.

Let's apply this template to define a module:

```
(function (root, factory) {
  if (typeof define === 'function' && define.amd) {
    define([], factory);
  } else if (typeof exports === 'object') {
    module.exports = factory();
  } else {
    root.returnExports = factory();
  }
}(this, function () {
  var pi = 3.14;

  function circumference(radius) {
    return 2*pi*radius;
  }

  function circleArea(radius) {
    return pi*radius*radius;
  }

  return {
    calculateCircumference:  circumference,
    calculateCircleArea:    circleArea
  };
}));
```

Once we define the module, we can use it on browsers not supporting AMD as follows:

```
console.log(returnExports.calculateCircumference(5));
```

If the browser has an AMD loader, we will load the module in the following way:

```
require(["geoModule"], function(geoModule) {
  console.log(geoModule.calculateCircumference(5));
});
```

Instead, in a CommonJS environment we will write:

```
var geoModule = require("./geoModule");

console.log(geoModule.calculateCircumference(5));
```

Dependency management

The previous example described how to define an UMD module without dependencies. If our module depends on another one, we can change the code as follows:

```
(function (root, factory) {
  if (typeof define === 'function' && define.amd) {
    // AMD. Register as an anonymous module.
    define(['module1'], factory);
  } else if (typeof exports === 'object') {
    // Node. Does not work with strict CommonJS, but
    // only CommonJS-like environments that support
    //module.exports, like Node.
    module.exports = factory(require('module1'));
  } else {
    // Browser globals (root is window)
    root.returnExports = factory(root.module1);
  }
}(this, function (module1) {
  //Module code
  return {...};
}));
```

The only difference compared to the previous code is the `module1` parameter and the string with the same name highlighted in bold.

The approach proposed is actually ugly and not so comfortable to use. Apart from the fact of being very verbose, the presence of dependencies forces us to adjust the code with the risk of introducing errors.

ECMAScript 6 modules

By what we have seen so far, organizing our JavaScript code in modules is not so simple. We must address various module definitions and different loading modes both not fully compatible. ECMAScript 6 specification proposes a standard solution to this problem offering native support for modules in a compact and effective way, quite a bit similar to the CommonJS module.

As per CommonJS, ES6 modules are stored in files. There is exactly one module per file and one file per module. We can export a functionality from a module using the `export` keyword. The following code shows a module exporting a function `myFunction()`, a class `myClass`, and a constant `myConst` using an approach called **named export**:

```
export function myFunction() {...};
export class myClass {...}
export const myConst = 123;
```

If the previous module is stored in a file named `myModule.js`, we can import one or more exported items using the `import` keyword:

```
import {myClass, myFunction} from "myModule";

myFunction();
```

In the preceding example, we imported the class `myClass` and the function `myFunction()`, that is, both items are inserted in the current scope. We can import all exported items using the following syntax:

```
import * as myModule from "myModule";

myModule.myFunction();
```

In this case, we associated the alias `myModule` to identify the imported module, so we use the exported items by prefixing them with the alias.

In the previous example, we exported multiple items by prefixing each of them with the `export` keyword. We can export items by grouping them as in the following:

```
function myFunction() {...};
class myClass {...}
const myConst = 123;

export {myFunction, myClass, myConst};
```

In this case, all the exported items are identified in a single statement and are bound to the `myModule` variable when imported.

When we want to export a single item, we can use the **default export** syntax:

```
export default function () {...}
```

In this example, we export a function, but it could be a class, setting it as the default export. A module can have a single default export, so this syntax is not exactly equivalent to a single named export. Note that there is no semicolon at the end of the default export item. In fact, the exported item is an anonymous declaration, not an expression.

We import a default export by mapping it to a name, as shown here:

```
import myFunction from "myModule";

myFunction();
```

The following code defines an ES6 version for our `geoModule`:

```
var pi = 3.14;

export function circumference(radius) {
    return 2*pi*radius;
}

export function circleArea(radius) {
    return pi*radius*radius;
}
```

We import only the `circumference()` function in the following way:

```
import {circumference} from "geoModule";

console.log(circumference(5));
```

A few important constraints must be taken into account when dealing with ES6 modules:

- The import and export of modules is static, that is, we cannot import or export module conditionally at runtime
- Imports are hoisted, that is, internally moved at the beginning of the current scope, so we can use an imported item even before the import statement
- The imported items are read only, that is, we cannot assign a new value outside the scope of the module that exports them

ES6 module loading

ECMAScript 6 modules are independent from the loading mode. It should work whether the engine loads modules synchronously or asynchronously. Even if its syntax is closer to the CommonJS syntax, and it may seem well suited for synchronous loading, asynchronous loading is enabled by the module's static structure. In fact, since module import is static and hoisted, an ES6 module loader can analyze which modules are imported by a module and load them before executing its body.

In order to enable asynchronous loading on browsers, we can use the `<module>` tag instead of the classic `<script>` tag. Currently, the `<module>` tag is just a proposal by Dave Herman published at `https://github.com/dherman/module-tag`. It is not yet included in the HTML5 specifications.

The following is an example of a module enclosed in the `<module>` tags:

```
<module>
  var pi = 3.14;

  export function circumference(radius) {
    return 2*pi*radius;
  }

  export function circleArea(radius) {
    return pi*radius*radius;
  }
</module>
```

In addition to the asynchronous loading, the `<module>` tag has its own scope and the variables declared inside the tag are local to that scope, while a declaration inside the `<script>` tag creates a global variable. Moreover, the code inside the `<module>` tag is implicitly in strict mode.

We can load external code in a browser using the `<module>` tag as in the following example:

```
<module import="geoModule"></module>
```

An alternative to the `<module>` tag for compatibility with legacy browsers that use polyfills is the following:

```
<script type="module" import="geoModule"></script>
```

An API to programmatically interact with the built-in module loader of a JavaScript engine is being defined. The WHATWG standard group proposed a specification of the module loader API at `http://whatwg.github.io/loader/`. This API allows us to customize module loader behavior by intercepting module loading and fetching modules on demand.

Summary

In this chapter, we discussed some ways to organize the code of a complex JavaScript application. We started by analyzing the global scope as a repository of shared data and agreed how it is better to minimize its use and to find a way to avoid name collisions. So, we introduced the concept of namespace and implemented it as object literals and as IIFE.

Then, we started to discuss the concept of module as the basic organizational unit that many languages supports natively. The lack of this construct in JavaScript before ECMAScript 6 specification has given rise to several proposals. We explored the module pattern, the classic approach based on the closure of an IIFE, and analyzed the various approaches in augmenting and combining modules. Then, we talked about the difference between script and module loading and discussed the two main paradigms to loading modules the CommonJS module and the Asynchronous Module Definition. We saw how these two approaches define incompatible module formats and are intended for different loading mode: the CommonJS approach is suitable for synchronous loading, typically for server-side applications, and AMD is designed for asynchronous loading, that is, browser applications. We also explained the attempt to create a bridge between the two paradigms through the Universal Module Definition.

Finally, we focused on the ECMAScript 6 module specification that actually is suitable for both synchronous and asynchronous loading modes and hopefully opens the way for the module's standardization in the JavaScript world.

In the next chapter, we will focus on the SOLID principles of object-oriented design.

11
SOLID Principles

Designing software is a tricky task. Often an application grows following the user's needs, and if it is poorly designed, sooner or later we will face troubles. The SOLID principles can help us to design better applications. They allow us to detect points of weakness and to write robust, flexible, and maintainable code. Even though SOLID principles were born for classical OOP languages, they can be applied to JavaScript language as well.

In this chapter, we will explore the SOLID principles by discussing the following topics:

- Single Responsibility Principle
- Open/Closed Principle
- Liskov Substitution Principle
- Interface Segregation Principle
- Dependency Inversion Principle

Principle of OOP design

When we discussed the Object-Oriented Programming principles in Chapter 2, *Diving into OOP Principles* we introduced association, aggregation, composition, encapsulation, inheritance, and polymorphism. These principles are the foundations of any language that can be defined as object oriented. Therefore, they are the basic principles without which we can not say that we are applying the OOP model.

However, the simple principles of OOP are not enough to guarantee us the creation of robust and easily maintainable applications. They simply provide us with tools that allow us to model a problem using abstractions we call objects. The robustness, maintainability, and flexibility of an application mainly depends on how we design it, decide to put together its components, and use the principles of OOP.

According to Robert C. Martin, one of the co-authors of the Agile Manifesto, there are three characteristics of bad design to be avoided:

- **Rigidity**: This is the difficulty of modifying an application because any change involves too many parts of the system
- **Fragility**: This is the generation of bugs in a part of an application due to changes in other parts of it
- **Immobility**: This is the inability to use a component in another software because it is too dependent on the current application

In order to avoid these issues, Martin suggests some design principles commonly known as SOLID.

SOLID is a mnemonic acronym that refers to a set of five principles at the base of a good software design:

- Single Responsibility Principle
- Open/Closed Principle
- Liskov Substitution Principle
- Interface Segregation Principle
- Dependency Inversion Principle

The application of these principles helps us to identify potential situations that put the design of our applications at risk.

Although, in general, these principles are related to the context of classical Object-Oriented Programming and refer to classes, types, and interfaces, the underlying concepts are also applicable to a dynamically typed and prototype-based language such as JavaScript. Let's start to analyze these principles and to learn how to apply them in the development of our applications one by one.

The Single Responsibility Principle

The first principle of the SOLID stack is the **Single Responsibility Principle**. Following Martin's definition, the principle says:

A class should have only one reason to change.

The attribution of single responsibility leads to misunderstanding this principle. In fact it is often mistakenly taken to mean that a class should only do one thing. The definition of the principle, however, states that the only reason for which a class or object should be changed is because it has changed its responsibility. So, it is not true that an object can only do one thing, rather it can do more things that belong to the same responsibilities. In other words, the actions assigned to an object must be consistent with the unique responsibility that was given. If there are two different reasons why an object or class must be changed, then we have to separate the two responsibilities into as many objects or classes.

Let's look at a practical example of this principle by introducing an order constructor function:

```
function Order(customerId) {
  this.customerId =  customerId;
  this.dateTime = new Date();
  this.items = [];
}
```

The structure of the order is minimal to enable us to focus on our goal—we have a customer identifier, an order date, and an array containing the list of items that are part of the order.

Let's look at the class responsible for order management:

```
var OrderManager = (function () {

  function OrderManager() {}

  OrderManager.prototype.createOrder = function (customerId) {
    this.order = new Order(customerId);
  };

  OrderManager.prototype.addItem = function (item) {
    this.order.items.push(item);
  };

  OrderManager.prototype.sendOrder = function () {
    if (this.isValid(this.order)) {
      var xhr = new XMLHttpRequest();
      xhr.onreadystatechange = function () {
        if (xhr.readyState == 4 && xhr.status == 200) {
          var response = JSON.parse(xhr.responseText);
          handleResponse(response);
        }
      };
      xhr.open("POST", "/api/orders");
      xhr.setRequestHeader("Content-Type", "application
      /json;charset=UTF-8");
```

```
      xhr.send(JSON.stringify(order));
    }
    else {
      handleError({ message: "Not valid order!" });
    }
  };

  OrderManager.prototype.isValid = function (order) {
    return order.items.length > 0;
  };

  return OrderManager;
}());
```

This constructor provides a number of methods to create a new order (createOrder()), to add an item to the order (addItem()), to validate the order (isValid()), and to send an order to the server (sendOrder()).

An example of use of OrderManager is as follows:

```
var orderMngr = new OrderManager();

orderMngr.createOrder(1234);
orderMngr.addItem({itemId: 111, description: "Item 111"});
orderMngr.sendOrder();
```

Analyzing the OrderManager constructor, we note that its main responsibility is to manage the order, as the name itself suggests. So its actions should be related to the order life cycle. If something changes in the way an order is managed, we expect to change the constructor's code in order to adapt it to the new management mode.

However, the sendOrder() method includes a responsibility that is not closely related to order management—we are talking about the actual sending of the order. In the example, the sendOrder() method takes care of sending the order to the server via an Ajax call to a specific URL. Suppose that at some point the approach to send the order to the server changes, not for reasons concerning the management order, but for technical reasons. For example, the server API specifications have changed or we no longer want to use XMLHttpRequest to send the request to the server but a third-party library. We identified a second reason to change the OrderManager constructor function. So, the constructor is breaking the Single Responsibility Principle because, in addition to the responsibility for managing the order, it also has the responsibility to take care of the technical details of sending the order to the server.

In order to apply the Single Responsibility Principle, the task of order sending must be assigned to another component. So, we define a new constructor that will take care of this responsibility:

```
var OrderSender = (function() {

  function OrderSender() {}

  OrderSender.prototype.send = function(order) {
    var xhr = new XMLHttpRequest();

    xhr.onreadystatechange = function () {
      if (xhr.readyState == 4 && xhr.status == 200) {
        var response = JSON.parse(xhr.responseText);
        handleResponse(response);
      }
    };

    xhr.open("POST", "/api/orders");
    xhr.setRequestHeader("Content-Type", "application
    /json;charset=UTF-8");
    xhr.send(JSON.stringify(order));
  }

  return  OrderSender;
})();
```

The `OrderSender` constructor has a unique method that performs the action that was previously carried out within the `sendOrder()` method of `OrderManager`. In other words, we moved to `OrderSender` a responsibility, which `OrderManager` had before.

We can rewrite `OrderManager` as shown here:

```
var OrderManager = (function () {

  function OrderManager() {}

  OrderManager.prototype.createOrder = function (customerId) {
    this.order = new Order(customerId);
  };

  OrderManager.prototype.addItem = function (item) {
    this.order.items.push(item);
  };

  OrderManager.prototype.sendOrder = function () {
    if (this.isValid(this.order)) {
```

```
      var orderSender = new OrderSender();
      orderSender.send(order);
    }
    else {
      handleError({ message: "Not valid order!" });
    }
  };

  OrderManager.prototype.isValid = function (order) {
    return order.items.length > 0;
  };

  return OrderManager;
}());
```

The highlighted code shows the difference over the previous code: `OrderManager` assigns to `OrderSender` the task of actually sending the order to the server. In this way, the only reason to modify the `OrderManager` constructor will be because something has changed in the order management.

Applying the Single Responsibility Principle, we create an application with a clear layered structure that allows us to reuse the business logic across multiple applications, and improve its maintainability and scalability.

The Open/Closed Principle

The second SOLID principle concerns the extensibility of components and is called the **Open/Closed Principle**. Its focus is on avoiding changes when we need to extend a component's feature. The principle states:

> *Software entities like classes, modules and functions should be open for extension but closed for modifications.*

In the design of the components of our application, we have to take into account these two aspects:

- **Open for extension**: The components should be adjustable to the changing needs of the application
- **Closed for modifications**: The required changes should not involve the original component itself

If we apply this principle, we can get more easily adaptable and maintainable applications.

To illustrate how to apply this principle, let's take the example of order management in the previous section with some small modifications:

```
function Order(customerId) {
  this.customerId =  customerId;
  this.dateTime = new Date();
  this.totalAmount = 0;
  this.items = [];
}

var OrderManager = (function () {

  function OrderManager() {}

  OrderManager.prototype.createOrder = function (customerId) {
    this.order = new Order(customerId);
  };

  OrderManager.prototype.addItem = function (item) {
    this.order.items.push(item);
    this.order.totalAmount = this.order.totalAmount + item.price;
  };

  OrderManager.prototype.sendOrder = function () {
    if (this.isValid(this.order)) {
      this.applyDiscount(this.order);
      var orderSender = new OrderSender();
      orderSender.send(order);
    }
    else {
      handleError({ message: "Not valid order!" });
    }
  };

  OrderManager.prototype.isValid = function (order) {
    return order.items.length > 0;
  };

  OrderManager.prototype.applyDiscount = function (order) {
    var itemsCount = order.items.length;
    var discountPercentage;
    if (itemsCount < 10) {
      discountPercentage = 0;
    } else {
      if (itemsCount < 20) {
        discountPercentage = 10;
      } else {
        if (itemsCount < 30) {
```

```
                discountPercentage = 30;
            } else {
                discountPercentage = 50;
            }
        }
    }
    order.totalAmount = order.totalAmount - order.totalAmount *
discountPercentage / 100;   };

    return OrderManager;
}());
```

We highlighted the new code with respect to the previous section. In summary, we added a total amount for the order and the possibility to apply a discount based on the count of items in the order. The `applyDiscount()` method examines the number of items in the order and applies a discount percentage accordingly to some quantity ranges: 0 to 9 items, 10 to 19 items, 20 to 29 items, and over 30 items.

Suppose we want to introduce a new discount level, for example, from 30 to 50 items. To do this, we need to change the `OrderManager` constructor breaking the Open/Closed Principle. How can we rewrite the constructor function so that the principle is respected?

Let's consider the following code:

```
function Order(customerId) {
    this.customerId =  customerId;
    this.dateTime = new Date();
    this.totalAmount = 0;
    this.items = [];
}


var OrderManager = (function () {
    var discounters = [];

    function OrderManager() {}

    OrderManager.prototype.createOrder = function (customerId) {
        this.order = new Order(customerId);
    };

    OrderManager.prototype.addItem = function (item) {
        this.order.items.push(item);
        this.order.totalAmount = this.order.totalAmount +        item.price;
    };

    OrderManager.prototype.sendOrder = function () {
```

```
    if (this.isValid(this.order)) {
      this.applyDiscount(this.order);
      var orderSender = new OrderSender();
      orderSender.send(order);
    }
    else {
      handleError({ message: "Not valid order!" });
    }
  };

  OrderManager.prototype.isValid = function (order) {
    return order.items.length > 0;
  };

  OrderManager.prototype.registerDiscounter =
    function(discounter) {
    discounters.push(discounter);
  };
  OrderManager.prototype.applyDiscount = function (order) {
    var i;    for (i=0; i < discounters.length; i++) {
      if (discounters[i].isApplicable(order)) {
       discounters[i].apply(order);
        break
      }
    }
  };

  return OrderManager;
}());
```

We've highlighted the changed code. Note the private `discounters` array definition that is populated by the `registerDiscounter()` method. This array is intended to contain one or more `discounter` objects that are responsible for applying a discount. We then redefined the `applyDiscount()` method, which no longer calculates the discount to be applied but delegates this task to the discounter. As we can see in the implementation of the `applyDiscount()` method, a `discounter` has a `isApplicable()` method, which checks whether the discount is applicable and an `apply()` method which applies the discount.

The following code shows how to implement the discount ranges seen before using the discounters:

```
var bronzeDiscounter = {
  isApplicable: function(order) {
    var itemsCount = order.items.length;

    return (itemsCount >= 10 && itemsCount < 20)
```

```
  },
  apply: function(order) {
    order.totalAmount = order.totalAmount - order.totalAmount * 10      /
100;
  }
};

var silverDiscounter = {
  isApplicable: function(order) {
    var itemsCount = order.items.length;

    return (itemsCount >= 20 && itemsCount < 30)
  },
  apply: function(order) {
    order.totalAmount = order.totalAmount - order.totalAmount * 30      /
100;
  }
};

var goldDiscounter = {
  isApplicable: function(order) {
    var itemsCount = order.items.length;

    return (itemsCount >= 30)
  },
  apply: function(order) {
    order.totalAmount = order.totalAmount - order.totalAmount * 50      /
100;
  }
};
```

Using this approach, we comply with the Open/Closed Principle since we can extend the functionality of the `OrderManager` constructor without changing it. In fact, to add a new discount range, it is sufficient to create a new discounter, register it through the `registerDiscounter()` method, and adjust if necessary other discounters, as in the following example:

```
var goldDiscounter = {
  isApplicable: function(order) {
    var itemsCount = order.items.length;

    return (itemsCount >= 30 && itemsCount < 50)
  },
  apply: function(order) {
    order.totalAmount = order.totalAmount - order.totalAmount * 40      /
100;
  }
```

```
};

var platinumDiscounter = {
  isApplicable: function(order) {
    var itemsCount = order.items.length;

    return (itemsCount >= 50)
  },
  apply: function(order) {
    order.totalAmount = order.totalAmount - order.totalAmount * 50      /
100;
  }
};


orderManager.registerDiscounter(goldDiscounter);
orderManager.registerDiscounter(platinumDiscounter);
```

As we can see, it will not be necessary to modify the `OrderManager` constructor.

The Liskov Substitution Principle

The third SOLID principle, the **Liskov Substitute Principle**, is somehow an extension of the Open/Closed Principle. In fact, it concerns the possibility of extending a component through inheritance and imposes a constraint that ensures interoperability of objects within an inheritance hierarchy. The principle says:

> *Subtypes must be substitutable for their base types.*

When we use inheritance, we extend a base component to create specialized components. The principle of Liskov invites us to be careful not to disrupt the functionality of the parent component when we define a derived component. Classes, objects, functions, and other software entities that have to do with the components of an inheritance hierarchy must be able to interact in a uniform manner. In other words, a derived component must be semantically equivalent to its base component. Otherwise, the new components can produce undesired effects when they interact with existing components.

 The Liskov Substitution Principle was introduced in 1987 by Barbara Liskov, an MIT professor, during the Conference on Object-Oriented Programming Systems Languages and Applications, in a paper called *Data abstraction and hierarchy*.

Let's try to explain this principle with an example. Consider the discounter objects seen in the previous section and define a constructor like the one shown here:

```
function Discounter(min, max, discountPercentage) {
  this.min = min;
  this.max = max;
  this.discountPercentage = discountPercentage;
}

Discounter.prototype.isApplicable = function(order) {
  var itemsCount = order.items.length;

  return (itemsCount >= this.min && itemsCount < this.max)
};

Discounter.prototype.apply = function(order) {
  order.totalAmount = order.totalAmount - order.totalAmount *
discountPercentage / 100;
};
```

In practice, we generalized the discounter features creating a constructor function, so we can define an instance as in the following example:

```
var bronzeDiscounter = new Discounter(10, 20, 10);
```

Now, if we want to define a new type of discount based on the amount of the order and not on the quantity of items, we may expand the `Discounter` constructor by simply changing the `isApplicable()` method, as shown here:

```
function AmountDiscounter(min, max, discountPercentage) {
  Discounter.apply(this, arguments);
}

AmountDiscounter.prototype.isApplicable = function(order) {
  var orderAmount = order.totalAmount;

  return (orderAmount >= min && orderAmount < max)
};
```

The change is very simple, but completely changes the semantics of the base constructor. The `AmountDiscounter` definition is in contrast to the `Discounter` definition and violates the Liskov Substitution Principle, since I cannot use an instance of `AmountDiscounter`, which currently uses an instance of `Discounter`. If we do that, the results would be unpredictable, since the old client assumes that a discounter works on quantity ranges, not on amount ranges.

The applicability of the Liskov principle is not simple. In fact, the extension of a component is not necessarily under our control, especially if our code is a library used by third parties. In these cases, the user can create derived objects and redefine functionalities at his own discretion, with the risk of infringing the principle of Liskov.

A strategy for limiting the possibility of violations of this principle is to limit the use of inheritance, when it is possible. The well-known suggestion of the Gang of Four says to *favor object composition over class inheritance*. In fact, in addition to the potential violation of the substitution principle of Liskov, inheritance creates coupling between the base and derived entities and the changes propagation can have effects not always so clear. In languages with static typing, it is usually suggested the definition of interfaces instead of the use of inheritance, but in dynamic languages like JavaScript, this suggestion is not relevant, since the interface of an object is not determined by the type of the object, but by the capabilities expected by the object itself.

Anyway, even if the Liskov principle refers to inheritance, its true essence is in the behavioral compatibility, that is, to maintain a uniform behavior for objects in a given category.

The Interface Segregation Principle

When designing the interface of an object, we should limit to define what is strictly necessary, avoiding carrying around stuff that is not used. This is, in a nutshell, the **Interface Segregation Principle**, whose official version says:

> *Clients should not be forced to depend on methods they do not use.*

Although JavaScript does not support interfaces as abstract types to define contracts through a typing system, as we saw in Chapter 5, *Defining Contracts with Duck Typing*, it may somehow be emulated through Duck Typing. In any case, this principle does not refer to the interfaces as a pure syntactic element, but to the whole set of public properties and methods of an object.

In the definition of our object interfaces, therefore, we should be careful to only define what actually is necessary. This avoids the exposure of members that could create ambiguity and confusion.

Let's consider the following code:

```
function Discounter(min, max, discountPercentage, gadget) {
  this.min = min;
  this.max = max;
```

```
    this.discountPercentage = discountPercentage;
    this.gadget = gadget;
}

Discounter.prototype.isApplicable = function(order) {
    var itemsCount = order.items.length;

    return (itemsCount >= this.min && itemsCount < this.max)
};

Discounter.prototype.apply = function(order) {
    order.totalAmount = order.totalAmount - order.totalAmount *
discountPercentage / 100;
};

Discounter.prototype.addGadget = function(order) {
    order.items.push(this.gadget);
}
```

We defined the `Discounter` constructor adding the gadget management. Using this definition all object instances will have the `gadgets` property and the `addGadget()` method, even if most of these objects will not use them. To comply with the Interface Segregation Principle, it would be appropriate to establish a special constructor for discounters that manage gadgets:

```
function GadgetDiscounter(min, max, gadget) {
    this.min = min;
    this.max = max;
    this.gadget = gadget;
}

GadgetDiscounter.prototype.isApplicable = function(order) {
    var itemsCount = order.items.length;

    return (itemsCount >= this.min && itemsCount < this.max)
};

GadgetDiscounter.prototype.addGadget = function(order) {
    order.items.push(this.gadget);
}
```

In this case, we defined a new constructor function `GadgetDiscounter` that has the `gadget` property and the `addGadget()` method. So, the discounters that add gadgets to the order are instances of this constructor.

A better solution is based on a mixin approach that allows us to augment the standard discounter interface, as shown here:

```
function Discounter(min, max, discountPercentage) {
  this.min = min;
  this.max = max;
  this.discountPercentage = discountPercentage;
}

Discounter.prototype.isApplicable = function(order) {
  var itemsCount = order.items.length;

  return (itemsCount >= this.min && itemsCount < this.max)
};

Discounter.prototype.apply = function(order) {
  order.totalAmount = order.totalAmount - order.totalAmount *
discountPercentage / 100;
};

var gadgetMixin = {
  gadget: {},
  addGadget: function(order) {
    order.items.push(this.gadget);
  }
};

var discounter = new Discounter(10, 20, 0);
var gadgetDiscounter = augment(discounter, gadgetMixin);

gadgetDiscounter.gadget = {name: "A nice gadget!"}
```

We defined the `gadgetMixin` object literal and used it to augment an instance of `Discounter`. `augment()`, the function we defined in `Chapter 4`, *Inheriting and Creating Mixins*, during the mixin discussion. This approach allows us to extend just the objects that really need the interface to work with gadgets.

As we have seen, the Interface Segregation Principle is quite similar to the Single Responsibility Principle. Both promote simplification and cohesion of the components; but while the Single Responsibility Principle refers to the component as a whole, the Interface Segregation Principle only requires simplification at the public interface level.

The Dependency Inversion Principle

The last SOLID principle concerns the dependence among the components of an application and states that:

1. High-level modules should not depend on low-level modules. Both should depend on abstractions.

2. Abstractions should not depend upon details. Details should depend on abstractions.

This is the **Dependency Inversion Principle**, and it consists of two recommendations. The first one concerns the classic layered architecture of an application, where in general the components of the high level are strictly dependent on the components at the low level. A possible modification to a low-level component may require a change to one or more high-level components. The first recommendation suggests to reverse this dependency, changing it toward an intermediate abstraction, such as an interface. So, a low-level component must implement an interface used by the components of the higher level.

The second recommendation says to make sure that the implementation details do not affect an abstraction. An abstraction, such as an interface, must describe a behavior and implementation details must follow the behavior defined by abstraction. The implementation can change without affecting the referred abstraction. In other words, if, for example, we defined an abstraction to access a persistence system, the implementation must comply with the abstraction, but its internal implementation can change at will.

Let's try to explain this principle with an example. Consider the code for order management:

```
function Order(customerId) {
  this.customerId =  customerId;
  this.dateTime = new Date();
  this.totalAmount = 0;
  this.items = [];
}


var OrderManager = (function () {
  var discounters = [];

  function OrderManager() {}

  OrderManager.prototype.createOrder = function (customerId) {
    this.order = new Order(customerId);
  };
```

```javascript
OrderManager.prototype.addItem = function (item) {
  this.order.items.push(item);
  this.order.totalAmount = this.order.totalAmount + item.price;
};

OrderManager.prototype.sendOrder = function () {
  if (this.isValid(this.order)) {
    this.applyDiscount(this.order);
    var orderSender = new OrderSender();
    orderSender.send(order);
  }
  else {
    handleError({ message: "Not valid order!" });
  }
};

OrderManager.prototype.isValid = function (order) {
 return order.items.length > 0;
};

OrderManager.prototype.registerDiscounter = function(discounter)     {
 discounters.push(discounter);
};

OrderManager.prototype.applyDiscount = function (order) {
  var i;

  for (i=0; i < discounters.length; i++) {
    if (discounters[i].isApplicable(order)) {
      discounters[i].apply(order);
      break
    }
  }
};

  return OrderManager;
}());

var OrderSender = (function() {

  function OrderSender() {}

  OrderSender.prototype.send = function(order) {
    var xhr = new XMLHttpRequest();

    xhr.onreadystatechange = function () {
      if (xhr.readyState == 4 && xhr.status == 200) {
        var response = JSON.parse(xhr.responseText);
```

```
            handleResponse(response);
         }
      };

      xhr.open("POST", "/api/orders");
      xhr.setRequestHeader("Content-Type", "application
  /json;charset=UTF-8");
      xhr.send(JSON.stringify(order));
   }

   return   OrderSender;
})();
```

In this example, we can see the dependence between the `OrderManager` and `OrderSender` constructors. We see that the body of the `sendOrder()` method creates a new instance of `OrderSender`. Any changes to the delivery mode of the order may require a change to `OrderManager`. For example, suppose that in addition to sending orders via HTTP we need to send certain types of orders via e-mail, we should change the `sendOrder()` method to include this possibility.

If we want to apply the Dependency Inversion Principle, we must ensure that `OrderManager` don't depend on the implementation details of order sending but, on the contrary, establish a common interface, the implementation of order sending must comply with this interface.

In our case, we implicitly determined that an object for sending an order should implement a `send()` method. So, we can solve the dependency problem as shown here:

```
function Order(customerId) {
   this.customerId =  customerId;
   this.dateTime = new Date();
   this.totalAmount = 0;
   this.items = [];
}


var OrderManager = (function () {
   var discounters = [];
   var orderSender;
   function OrderManager(sender) {
      orderSender = sender;
   }

   OrderManager.prototype.createOrder = function (customerId) {
      this.order = new Order(customerId);
   };
```

```
OrderManager.prototype.addItem = function (item) {
  this.order.items.push(item);
  this.order.totalAmount = this.order.totalAmount + item.price;
};

OrderManager.prototype.sendOrder = function () {
  if (this.isValid(this.order)) {
    this.applyDiscount(this.order);
    orderSender.send(order);
  }
  else {
    handleError({ message: "Not valid order!" });
  }
};

OrderManager.prototype.isValid = function (order) {
  return order.items.length > 0;
};

OrderManager.prototype.registerDiscounter = function(discounter)    {
  discounters.push(discounter);
};

OrderManager.prototype.applyDiscount = function (order) {
  var i;

  for (i=0; i < discounters.length; i++) {
    if (discounters[i].isApplicable(order)) {
      discounters[i].apply(order);
      break
    }
  }
};

return OrderManager;
}());


var HttpOrderSender = (function() {

function OrderSender() {}

OrderSender.prototype.send = function(order) {
  var xhr = new XMLHttpRequest();

  xhr.onreadystatechange = function () {
    if (xhr.readyState == 4 && xhr.status == 200) {
      var response = JSON.parse(xhr.responseText);
```

```
            handleResponse(response);
        }
    };

    xhr.open("POST", "/api/orders");
    xhr.setRequestHeader("Content-Type", "application
/json;charset=UTF-8");
    xhr.send(JSON.stringify(order));
    }

    return  OrderSender;
})();
```

As usual, the highlighted code shows the differences compared to the previous solution. In this case, we defined a `orderSender` variable representing the component responsible for the order sending, no matter what approach is used for sending. This component is not created within the `sendOrder()` method, but it is passed as a parameter to the `OrderManager` constructor or, as they say, is injected into the `OrderManager` constructor. We then renamed the constructor function that sends orders via HTTP in `HttpOrderSender`, just to distinguish it from any other components that implement the same interface `send()`. The following instructions explain how to inject the sender component into the `OrderManager`:

```
var  httpOrderSender = new  HttpOrderSender();
var orderManager = new OrderManager(httpOrderSender);
```

With this approach, we reversed the dependency between `OrderManager` and `OrderSender` using a technique called **dependency injection**.

Dependency inversion, inversion of control, and dependency injection

Often, there is confusion between dependency inversion, inversion of control, and dependency injection. The three concepts are somehow connected, but they are not exactly the same thing. We will try to make things clearer.

Dependency inversion is a software design principle, the last principle of the SOLID stack. As we said in this section, it states how two components should depend on each other and suggests that high-level components should not depend on low level components. It does not say how to do it or which technique to use.

A possible approach to make high-level components independent from low-level components is **inversion of control**, that is a way to apply the Dependency Inversion Principle. Inversion of control is the actual mechanism using which we can use to make the higher level components depend on abstractions rather than concrete implementation of lower level components.

 Inversion of control is sometimes jokingly called the **Hollywood Principle**. This name is borrowed from the cinema industry, where, after an auditions for a role in a Hollywood movie, usually the director says, *don't call us, we'll call you*. This sentence embodies the spirit of inversion of control.

Dependency injection is a technique to implement inversion of control. It injects the concrete implementation of a low-level component into a high-level component. So, dependency injection concretely applies the Dependency Inversion Principle in the software development by moving the binding of abstraction and concrete implementation out of the dependent component.

Dependency injection approaches

Independent of the language used, dependency injection can be done using three approaches:

- Constructor injection
- Method injection
- Property injection

The most common approach is the **constructor injection**. It is based on passing the dependency as a parameter of the constructor function. This is the approach we used in our example:

```
var  httpOrderSender = new  HttpOrderSender();
var orderManager = new OrderManager(httpOrderSender);
```

We created an `httpOrderSender` object and injected it into the `orderManager` object by passing it to the `OrderManager()` constructor function.

The constructor injection is suitable when the same dependency is valid for all the object's lifetime. In other words, if the `orderManager` object will use `httpOrderSender` during its life, the constructor injection approach is appropriate.

If we need to pass different dependencies on every method call, then we use **method injection**. For example, if we want to specify a different way of sending an order when we call the `sendOrder()` method, we can use the Method injection:

```
var  httpOrderSender = new  HttpOrderSender();
var orderManager = new OrderManager();
orderManager.sendOrder(httpOrderSender);
```

The **property injection** approach allows us to specify the dependency by assigning it to a property of the object. This gives the flexibility of changing dependency during the lifetime of the object and at the same time avoids having to specify the dependency for each method's call. We could apply this approach in our example as follows:

```
var  httpOrderSender = new  HttpOrderSender();
var orderManager = new OrderManager();

orderManager.sender =  httpOrderSender;
orderManager.sendOrder();
```

Here, we introduced the `sender` property to which we attached the `httpOrderSender` object. This object will be taken into account when the `sendOrder()` method is called.

Summary

In this chapter, we analyzed the SOLID principles, a set of five OOP Design principles that help to create more scalable and maintainable software. Although these principles were born for classical OOP languages, they are suitable also for a dynamic language such as JavaScript. In order to show this, we explored the five principles by providing examples of their application in JavaScript.

We saw that the Single Responsibility Principle is about designing software architecture with components that have a clear and simple behavior.

The Open/Closed Principle is about class design and feature extensions.

The Liskov Substitution Principle is about subtyping and inheritance.

The Interface Segregation Principle is about interface definition exposed to clients.

The Dependency Inversion Principle concerns the management of dependency among the application's components.

In the next chapter, we will continue the design topic by exploring modern architectures of JavaScript applications.

12
Modern Application Architectures

When the complexity of an application grows, we cannot write code without a well-defined structure that gives solidity and robustness and guarantees long-term maintainability. Without such structure, our project may collapse because we lose control over the code, and it becomes more and more complex, unreadable, and unchangeable. The structure we need is an architecture that combines together the various components of a piece of software, in order to satisfy the explicit and implicit requirements of a software project.

Architecture evolves with technology, and this is particularly true in the web context. So, when we search the right architecture for the goals of our project, we should take into account which architecture is suitable with a certain technology.

In this chapter, we will explore the main architectures for modern JavaScript applications and will analyze how they work and which benefits they provide. During the discussion, we will analyze a couple of design patterns that allows us to implement a fundamental feature that any architecture should aim—loose coupling.

We will discuss the following topics:

- Goals of an application architecture
- From traditional web applications to Single Page Applications
- The Zakas/Osmani architecture for scalable applications
- The facade and mediator patterns
- The cross-cutting features implementation
- The isomorphic applications

From scripts to applications

The growing role of JavaScript in application development is clear to everyone. Once it was a simple language to add interactivity to HTML pages, now the role of JavaScript has become increasingly important enough to completely overturn the relationship with HTML, its historical partner. In fact, a few years ago, web applications were primarily HTML markup with the addition of some JavaScript scripts; today, the majority of complex applications are represented by JavaScript code that controls the HTML markup generation and display.

Even outside of the web browser context, the role of JavaScript is increasing. Today, a JavaScript application is able to run on servers, desktop applications, mobile devices, and even on embedded systems.

This evolution gives JavaScript more responsibility than it had, when its role was mostly about interactivity management and posting data to the server. What used to be a collection of simple scripts has now become a complex combination of components that interact with each other to perform a certain job—it has become an application.

What is a large-scale application?

Of course, an application requires a certain organization with respect to a collection of scripts. Indeed, while in most cases each script is limited to exercising its mission and possibly interacting with other scripts, an application requires a greater coordination among the components, a centralized management features such as error handling, logging, and so on. This responsibility, along with others, becomes more evident when an application grows and becomes large.

But what exactly is a large-scale application?

The answer to this question is quite subjective, since in most cases it depends on the experience of the single developer. Some people associate the size to the number of lines of code, others combine the number of features or components involved. In any case, it is difficult to give an objective definition of what actually is a very large application.

A definition with which I can agree with is that provided by Addy Osmani:

> *Large-scale JavaScript apps are non-trivial applications requiring significant developer effort to maintain, where most heavy lifting of data manipulation and display falls to the browser.*

Although Osmani's definition explicitly refers to web applications, I think that it can be considered valid for any type of application. The key point is that the size of an application does not depend on a specific number of a technical application's elements, but on the **effort required for its maintenance**, that is from an activity in the future. The size of an application essentially depends on its complexity and the energy required to meet future requests for change. So this is not a scientific measurement, but yet another subjective point of view. However, it emphasizes a fundamental aspect of programming—the software changes over time.

With this basic assumption, we have to design our application so that it has a structure that can make our life easier in future developments. In other words, we need to define an architecture for our applications.

What is an application architecture?

The architecture of an application is the definition of its structure and the design of the interactions between its components decided according to specific project goals. It is very important to note that an application's architecture is determined not only by its features, but also by the project's cross requirements, such as performance, extensibility, maintainability, security, reusability, and so on. This means that there is no universal architecture, an architecture valid for any application. There are specific architectures for specific requirements. However, we have architectural patterns used in several common scenarios from which we can be inspired to choose a model for our application. As an example, the most common architectural patterns include the client/server architecture, the layered architecture, the service-oriented architecture, and so on. Of course, these are very general architectural patterns. More specific architectural pattern helps us to structure our applications in a more targeted way, as we will see later in this chapter.

Goals of an architecture design

Usually architecture decisions for an application are among the most difficult aspects to modify over time and have long-term consequences on an application's life. For this reason, it is necessary to define the architecture of an application accurately and wisely, trying to balance the three categories of requirements that usually drive a software project:

- **User or customer requirements**: Generally, these features and their usability are to be implemented, but may include any other constraints explicitly declared by the customer or user.
- **Business requirements**: This category includes requirements concerning the project's cost-effectiveness, both as per the first release and subsequent evolution and maintenance; some constraints, such as access to specific features based on a license, fall also into this category of requirements.
- **System requirements**: These requirements are related to the hardware and software platform on which the application will run and any constraints on deployment.

The satisfaction of these three categories of requirements must be taken into account when choosing a specific architecture for our application.

From old-style to Single Page Applications

Web applications are the best known application types involving JavaScript. Since its appearance, JavaScript and web browsers have established a lasting symbiosis that still holds, although with slightly different roles than in the past. In this context, in fact, we have seen a growing responsibility of JavaScript whose evolution, together with the evolution of HTML, has led us to create applications with an interaction model and an architecture very similar to desktop applications.

Old-style web applications

The traditional architecture of the early web applications consisted (and still consists) of a set of HTML pages, representing the user interface, with JavaScript scripts whose main task was managing the user interaction and rendering some graphic effects. As a part of this architecture, the transition from one screen to the next one implied a request to the server and a whole page loading, with obvious latency, especially if the page was very rich in content (graphics, text, and scripts).

The following diagram shows the interaction between the client and the server in an hypothetical form data submission:

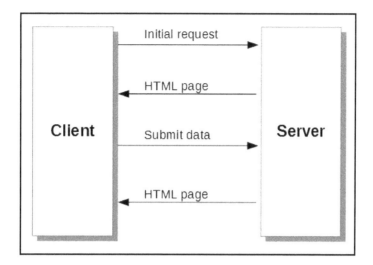

Single Page Applications

With Ajax and the new dynamic nature of the DOM, that is the ability to manipulate it at runtime via JavaScript, a new understanding of a web application was born. No longer a collection of pages whose navigation depends on the server, but a set of views under JavaScript's control on the client—**Single Page Applications** or **SPA** were born.

Single Page Applications are able to redraw any part of the user interface without requiring a server round-trip to retrieve HTML. This is achieved by separating the data from its presentation and usually applying some variant of MVC design pattern on the client. In fact, in the traditional approach to designing web applications, the client had the role of displaying the View and manage user's interaction, while the server implemented the Controller and the Model, as depicted in the following diagram:

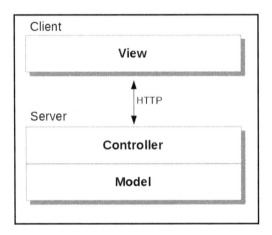

In Single Page Applications, the View and the Controller are implemented into the client, while the server acts as the Model:

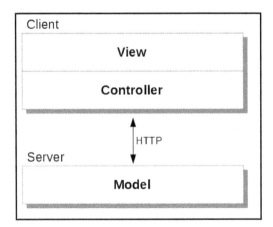

The server role

While in traditional web applications, the transition from one screen to another triggered the loading of a new HTML page from the server. In an SPA the server has no role in determining the screen transition. The client composes application views out of HTML templates and data, both of which it requests asynchronously as it needs them.

So, in the SPA model the server has no UI logic nor maintains any UI state. The role of the server consists in providing resources to the client, starting with the initial HTML for the single web page containing the entire application. The other resources are obtained in response to Ajax requests for data, represented usually by JSON data; but, they can be of different type such as HTML or even JavaScript code. The following picture describes the interactions between the client and the server:

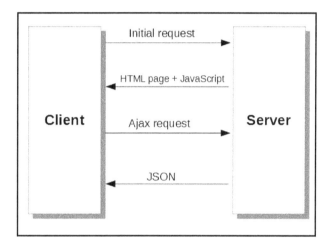

View composition

A Single Page Application is fully loaded in the initial page load and then dynamically updated with new HTML fragments composed by the client upon data loaded from the server. These fragments, usually called Views, make up what users commonly call screens or pages. A View can be a portion of the HTML page, such as a div or the entire screen. When a View occupies the entire screen, we call that a page to reflect the fact that it completely draws the user's attention, but technically it is just another view composed by the client.

We typically have many views in a SPA, and the resources needed to compose them are incrementally loaded from the server on demand. Since updating Views occurs asynchronously without reloading the entire page, Single Page Applications are more responsive and reduce network traffic and optimize its latency.

Navigation and routing

All modern SPA frameworks support the concept of routing. Routing is the ability to map URLs to Views so that users may navigate within the application's UI. Usually, it is implemented through a service called **router**. The main task of a router is to define how a URL is mapped to a View and to perform the transition between Views in response to a click on some menu item or any user action. If the user has not seen the requested View before, the application may make an HTTP request to the server in order to retrieve the resources and dynamically compose the View. Instead, if the View has already been viewed at least once, the browser may have cached it and the router will be smart enough not to make the HTTP request to the server. This approach helps to reduce round-tripping to and from a server and improve perceived performance.

The remote data

A Single Page Application requests data over HTTP from a server. Usually, we think of data as structured information such as a list of values. From a Single Page Application point of view, data can be different kinds of information: JSON, HTML, or any other resource that the application requires, even JavaScript code. In fact, an SPA can be designed so that its first load into the browser does not contain the entire application, but just the minimum code required to start properly. The rest of the code is dynamically loaded on demand during the user's navigation. Usually, JavaScript code is organized in modules loaded asynchronously using an AMD loader.

In other words, the data that a SPA requires can be anything the application needs from the server in order to build its Views. So, maybe the term data is not so appropriate, and we should instead use the term resource.

The Zakas/Osmani architecture

Although the Single Page Application architecture defines the key elements on which a web application that is responsive and efficient should rely, it does not say exactly how to organize our code or how to interact with the components that make up a complex application. We can say that the architecture of an SPA mainly proposes a model of interaction between client and server and suggests how to update the user interface, without saying how to organize the application's code.

An interesting architecture for large JavaScript applications is the one proposed by Nicholas C. Zakas and Addy Osmani. In contrast to the SPA, the main architectural goal of Zakas and Osmani is to organize the code so that the resulting application is easily maintainable and scalable. The architectural focus is mainly on the basis of SOLID principles we examined in `Chapter 11`, *SOLID Principles*. However, it is not in opposition to Single Page Applications, but it is neutral with respect to the navigation model and interaction with the server. Therefore, the Zakas/Osmani architecture can be adopted both for SPA and for traditional multipage applications. Indeed, we can say that this architecture can be considered valid also for languages other than JavaScript, and for contexts different from the web.

 The architecture we are describing was defined by Zakas and then revisited by Osmani. Their work can be found at the following URLs:

- `http://www.slideshare.net/nzakas/scalable-javascript-application-architecture`
- `https://addyosmani.com/largescalejavascript/`

Let's see in detail what's on this architecture.

The overall architecture

The Zakas/Osmani architecture relies on a set of loosely coupled components organized as shown in the following diagram:

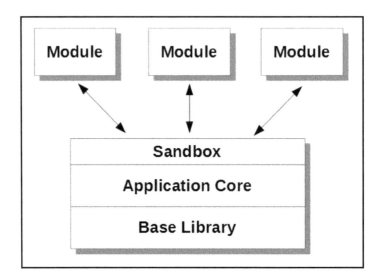

The proposed architecture contains a number of components each with a specific role and with a well-defined relationship between them. Each member knows little or nothing about the other components. The entire application is like a puzzle in which each piece has its own role but no one has an overall view of the final result. This is in line with the Single Responsibility Principle, according to which a component must have one goal and one reason to change.

Let's look at the role of each component of the architecture.

The modules

A **module** is an autonomous functional component and fully independent from the rest of the application. It contains both functional logic and portions of user interface and is focused on a single goal, according to the Single Responsibility Principle. We can think of it as a combination of JavaScript, HTML, and CSS that can be displayed on a portion of the web page, roughly corresponding to a view in the SPA model. In contexts different from the web, we can imagine a module as a logical unit that provides functionality on a specific aspect of the business logic.

Do not confuse the concept of module in the architecture proposed by Zakas and Osmani with module intended as a mechanism to isolate and combine application code. Zakas used the term module to create an analogy with the modules that make up the international space station: independent elements created by different people in different places and assembled together to build an organic unit.

The modules are components that know how to do their own jobs well and do not know anything about the rest of the application. A series of rules define the context in which they can operate:

- They cannot directly interact with other modules
- They can only interact with the sandbox
- They can only access the DOM portion under its control
- They cannot create global objects

A module has its own life cycle determined by the application core that decides when to create and destroy it. A module should be self-contained and independent from other modules in the application. It can fail and be removed without breaking the application. It can be changed with another module that implements the same interface without breaking the application.

It is possible to create a base module from which other modules can inherit, but in this case, it is recommended to keep the inheritance chain very short. A module should be very light and have as little dependency as possible. The lower the dependency between modules, the greater the flexibility and maintainability.

The Sandbox

We discussed the fact that a module is a self-contained unit and cannot directly communicate with other modules. The only way to communicate with the rest of the application is to use the Sandbox. The **Sandbox** is a layer that exposes a common API to interact with the other components of the application. It has the role of keeping the modules loosely coupled. In fact, by limiting the dependency of each module to a single component, it is easier to remove or replace a module in the application architecture. In addition, the Sandbox can carry out safety checks on the interaction requests toward the rest of the application, preventing unauthorized activities.

It is possible to create a specific Sandbox for each module or one Sandbox shared among all modules. This is an architectural choice that may depend on the degree of complexity of the internal API of the application. What all the Sandboxes must provide is a standard API for common tasks that a module can perform, such as:

- The communication with other modules
- The execution of Ajax requests
- Access to the DOM
- The association and disassociation of event handlers

The key thing to keep in mind is that a Sandbox does not implement any of the preceding features. It is simply an interface to the features implemented by the application core. The existence of this level in the architecture proposed by Zakas and Osmani ensures a decoupling between the implementation of internal services and the interface exposed to the modules, thus promoting an evolution of the application without upheavals. A typical Design Pattern to implement the Sandbox is the facade pattern.

The facade pattern

The purpose of the **facade pattern** is to provide an interface to filter interactions with one or more components in a system. Its use is quite common and the reasons to prevent direct access to the components can be various:

- Providing a simplified interface for access to a complex subsystem
- Providing a consistent interface with the rest of the application
- Reducing the coupling between the components

In the definition of a Sandbox, the main reason to use the facade pattern is essentially the last one, that is, reducing the coupling between the various application modules and between the modules and basic functionality.

The actors involved in the facade pattern are:

- **One or more clients**: These are the components that need to access one or more application subsystems
- **The facade**: It is the component providing access to the subsystems
- **One or more subsystems**: These are the application components the client wants to access to

The following diagram graphically shows the interactions between the components involved in the pattern:

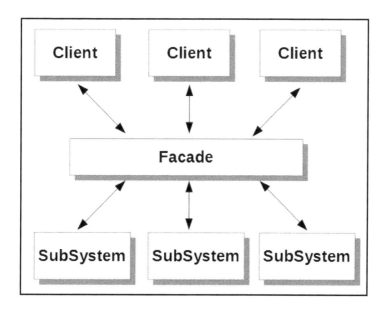

Let's look at an example of facade pattern implementation that aims to reduce coupling between components. Consider the following code:

```
function Facade() {}

Facade.prototype.getElement = function(selector) {
    return document.querySelector(selector);
};
```

We defined a constructor function for objects with the getElement() method. This method uses the querySelector() method to retrieve a DOM element. In this case, the wrapped subsystem is just the DOM. A client may use this method in the following way:

```
var facade = new Facade();
var myElement = facade.getElement(".class");
```

At first glance, the facade might look unnecessarily redundant. Why do we need an intermediate component when we can directly use the `querySelector()` method? However, the usefulness of the facade becomes evident if we think that we may change the access mode to DOM elements without affecting the clients. For example, suppose that for some reason we no longer use `querySelector()` to access DOM elements, but we want to use jQuery. This change only involves the facade and has no impact on clients.

In addition, in the architecture we are examining, accessing the DOM through the facade allows us to carry out special checks, such as checking if the client is authorized to access that portion of the DOM.

The application core

The **application core** is the central part of the application. It is the only global object in the entire application and includes in its basic tasks:

- Allowing registration of the modules
- Managing the life cycle of the modules
- Managing the communication between the modules
- Managing the interaction with the base library
- Handling errors

The application core should not be contacted directly by the modules, but only through the Sandbox. The Sandbox must be the only component able to contact the application core, and it must be the only component able to interact with the base library. Keeping these components separate enables us to easily swap out just one component with minimal impact on the others.

The application core has to be designed for extensibility so that it should be easy to add new features and extend existing ones with little effort. This ensures the evolution of the application and its maintainability.

The mediator pattern

The application core plays a crucial role in managing the communication between modules. To ensure independence between the modules, the application core allows them to communicate by implementing the **mediator pattern**. In this pattern, we have the following actors:

- **Colleagues**: These are two or more components that want to communicate
- **Mediator**: This is the component that enables communication among the colleagues

A graphic representation of the pattern is shown here:

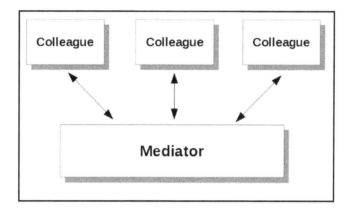

The colleagues who wish to communicate through the Mediator, register themselves and implement a common interface to send and receive messages. The Mediator keeps track of participants in the communication and deals with the exchange of messages. Let's see how to implement a sample Mediator by analyzing the following code:

```
var Mediator = function() {

  var colleagues = {};

  return {
    register: function(colleague) {
    colleagues[colleague.name] =  colleague;
    colleague.mediator = this;
    },

    send: function(message, sender, receiver) {
      if (receiver) {
        receiver.receive(message, sender);
```

```
      } else {
        for (key in colleagues) {
          if (colleagues[key] != sender) {
            colleagues[key].receive(message, sender);
          }
        }
      }
    }
  };
};
```

We can see that the private object `colleagues` keeps track of the participants, which can register via the `register()` method. The `send()` method allows us to send messages to a specific colleague or to all colleagues.

An example of a colleague will have the following definition:

```
var Colleague = function(name) {
  this.name = name;
  this.mediator = null;
};

Colleague.prototype.send = function(message, receiver) {
  this.mediator.send(message, this, receiver);
};

Colleague.prototype.receive = function(message, sender) {
  //process the message
};
```

With this infrastructure, if a colleague wants to participate in the communication, he can register as shown here:

```
var mediator = new Mediator();
var johnSmith = new Colleague("John");

mediator.register(johnSmith);
```

It can communicate with a specific colleague in the following way:

```
johnSmith.send("Hello!", marioRossi);
```

It can communicate with all colleagues using the following statement:

```
johnSmith.send("Hello!");
```

So, the Mediator deals with the indirect interaction of colleagues. The pattern is pretty generic and does not impose restrictions on the interaction modes between the components of a system. Its complexity can grow following the interaction policy between the components and communication approaches should be carefully analyzed. In the example we presented, the communication between the components is synchronous, but we might need asynchronous communication or a message queue or other approaches.

This generic nature of the mediator pattern leads us to consider, for example, the publisher/subscriber pattern that we saw in `Chapter 8`, *Data Binding*, as a special case of mediator where the communication is one way. Indeed, we can assimilate the role of observable with the mediator, while the role of the colleagues matches the subject and observer. In this case, only the subject generates messages, while only the observers receive them.

The base library

The bottom layer of the Zakas/Osmani architecture is the base library. This is the layer on which the entire application is built and provides general functionalities, independent from the specific application, such as:

- DOM manipulation
- Data serialization and deserialization
- Ajax communication
- Browser normalization and abstraction

These features can be provided by a custom or a standard library. The important point is that only the application core knows which libraries are being used and their replacement has an impact only on it and not on the rest of the application.

Cross-cutting features and AOP

When we introduced the SOLID principles in `Chapter 11`, *SOLID Principles*, we discussed the Single Responsibility Principle. Based on this principle, a component must be focused on a single responsibility, that is, it has to implement the features that concern only a single aspect of the application. Often, however, in a complex application, we need cross-cutting features that can be intrusive and forced to enter in a component some code that is not strictly correlated with its specific goal. These features include, the following:

- Error handling

- Logging and tracing
- Authorization control
- Transaction control

These and other features are usually included in any application, but in most cases, they tend to pollute the code introducing unrelated logic.

The log management example

Let's analyze this problem with an example. Suppose we have a constructor function for objects having a method that makes the sum of two numbers:

```
function Calculator() {}

Calculator.prototype.sum = function(x, y) {
    var result =  x + y;

    return result;
};
```

Now, imagine you want to log the execution of the method by tracing the input parameters and its result. We need to change the preceding code as in the following example:

```
function Calculator() {}

Calculator.prototype.sum = function(x, y) {
  console.log("Calling sum on " + x + " and " + y);
  var result =  x + y;

  console.log("Result of sum is " + result);
  return result;
};
```

This change, in addition to violating the Single Responsibility Principle, makes the code more complex and less maintainable.

Using inheritance

Can we use any different approach to avoid modifying the method's code? One approach might be to use the inheritance and create a derived version of our calculator:

```
function LoggedCalculator() {
  Calculator.apply(this, arguments);
```

```
    }

    LoggedCalculator.prototype.sum = function(x, y) {
        console.log("Calling sum on " + x + " and " + y);
        var result =  Calculator.prototype.sum(x, y);

        console.log("Result of sum is " + result);
        return result;
    };
```

The `LoggedCalculator()` constructor allows us to achieve the desired result without having to change the code of the base constructor `Calculator()`. However, all the clients of the `Calculator` instances must use the `LoggedCalculator()` constructor, turning the generation of log back an intrusive problem.

The Aspect-Oriented Programming approach

A solution to handle such a problem is to use the approach proposed by **Aspect-Oriented Programming** (AOP), a programming paradigm to increase the functionality of software entities (objects, methods, and so on.) without being intrusive. From a conceptual point of view, the AOP allows adding behavior to the existing code from the outside, without modifying the code itself.

Let's see how we can apply an AOP approach to our calculator example by analyzing the following code:

```
    var originalSum = Calculator.prototype.sum;

    Calculator.prototype.sum = function(x, y) {
        console.log("Calling sum on " + x + " and " + y);
        var result =  originalSum(x, y);

        console.log("Result of sum is " + result);
        return result;
    };
```

The technique described here is to replace the original method with a method that also logs messages. With this arrangement, we do not need to modify the original method nor to modify the code that uses the method.

At the time of writing, among the proposals included in a future ECMAScript specification (probably ES8) there are decorators. These are expressions that we can add to the definition of a property, a class or an object literal, that modifies the original definition. The introduction of this syntactic element significantly simplifies the adoption of an AOP approach in the management of cross-cutting features.

Isomorphic applications

One of the latest proposals as part of the possible architectures for JavaScript applications are the so-called **isomorphic applications**. The basic idea is to exploit the ability to execute JavaScript code both on server side and client side, being able to obtain benefits both in terms of performance and code reuse.

 There have been some discussions on whether to use the term Isomorphic to describe the ability to run a JavaScript application on both the client and the server. In particular, the issue was raised in the juxtaposition of the term to the language—Isomorphic JavaScript. Alternatively, the term universal JavaScript was proposed, but at present it does not seem to have had much success.
More on the topic, you can find on the following posts:
`https://medium.com/@ghengeveld/isomorphism-vs-universal-j avascript-4b47fb481beb`
`https://medium.com/@mjackson/universal-javascript-4761051 b7ae9`

In the Single Page Application architecture, the initial request from the browser causes the download of the JavaScript application before it can be rendered in the first screen. The waiting time may be long depending on the size of the application, its complexity, the computing capacity of the device, and the speed of the network connection. The isomorphic applications intend to overcome these limitations by proposing a hybrid approach between traditional web applications and Single Page Applications.

The ability to run the same application on both the server and the client offers new scenarios:

- The server can immediately send the rendering of the first page of the application, while in the background the client can download the entire application, optimizing the initial load time
- The server can send the result of page rendering as in traditional web applications, according to the type of client, such as clients that do not have sufficient computing resources or web crawlers for SEO optimizations
- We can also simply share libraries used in both server-side and client-side processing

Of course, this scenario brings new technical challenges, such as the uniform management of the routing on the server and on the client or the HTML markup rendering even without a DOM, as it happens on the server. For the management of these aspects ad hoc framework, such as Meteor or Rendr, should be exploited.

Summary

In this chapter, we explored some concepts about modern architectures for JavaScript applications. We started analyzing the evolution of JavaScript and the growth of its role not only for web applications but also for other kinds of applications that can run on various environments. We analyzed the main principles that any architecture must follow in order to get not only a working application, but also to be extensible and maintainable.

We compared old-style web application with Single Page Application architectures and showed the peculiarities and benefits. Then, we described the Zakas/Osmani architecture for scalable JavaScript applications. This architecture tries to apply the SOLID principles in order to create applications that are easier to maintain, thanks to a clear separation of concerns. We examined the components of the architecture and the patterns that can be used to reduce coupling. In particular, we introduced the facade pattern and the mediator pattern.

We also discussed how cross-cutting features such as logging, authorization checks, and similar jobs should be implemented. We suggested to use techniques inspired by the Aspect-Oriented Programming paradigm. So, we closed the chapter with a hint on the Isomorphic Applications, that is, applications that can be run on the client and on the server.

This chapter concludes the book, in which we have seen how JavaScript can implement the Object-Oriented Programming principles, even if with its peculiarities. We explored various programming techniques and the most commonly used design patterns in the development of JavaScript applications.

The scope of the language is increasingly expanding, ranging from web to mobile, desktops, and embedded applications. We are sure that programming with JavaScript will be even more interesting in the coming years and understanding how to apply the Object-Oriented Programming paradigm will be very useful.

Index

www.ingramcontent.com/pod-product-compliance
Lightning Source LLC
Chambersburg PA
CBHW060520060326
40690CB00017B/3336